N̶i̶m̶r̶o̶d̶ ̶I̶n̶t̶e̶rⁿational Journal

REVISITED

THE UNIVERSITY OF TULSA
TULSA, OKLAHOMA

ISSN 0029-053X

ISBN 0-9720993-3-6

Volume 47 Number 2

Spring/Summer 2004

Nimrod International Journal IS INDEXED IN THE AMERICAN HUMANITIES INDEX

Acknowledgments

The advisory and editorial boards of *Nimrod International Journal* are grieved at the loss of their friend, Ruth G. Hardman, whose heart and mind guided us through over 25 years of our publication. *Nimrod*'s Awards 26, October 2004, will be dedicated to her memory, with an article describing Mrs. Hardman's extensive contribution to *Nimrod* and to literature in Oklahoma and the world.

    This issue of *Nimrod* is funded by donations, subscriptions, and sales. *Nimrod* and The University of Tulsa acknowledge with gratitude the many individuals and organizations that support *Nimrod*'s publication, annual prize, and outreach programs: *Nimrod*'s Advisory and Editorial Boards; and *Nimrod*'s Angels, Benefactors, Donors, and Patrons.

TABLE OF CONTENTS

BEYOND

Francine Ringold
Vietnam Revisited/America Rediscovered

Writers are always revisiting the past and trying to decipher the present. If we are diligent and lucky, we make discoveries; we reshape and endow a future. In the best of our poetry and prose, we have a conversation not only with ourselves but also with the world. In this issue, *Nimrod* offers not only Vietnam, past and present, but a section entitled *Beyond*, poetry and prose, accepted from submissions to *Nimrod* during the past year in keeping with our open submission policy, that crosses boundaries of time and tradition.

"Vietnam Revisited" moves from *Tradition*, John Balaban's exquisite translations of *ca dao*, folk poems carried on the wind and recorded under conical hats that umbrella the centuries, to the modern Vietnamese poet Lê Pham Lê's original poems that sensitively reflect an earlier time and a modern predicament. The fable, "The Mountain of Waiting," that follows, bears the stamp of the French occupation of Vietnam, but also of an archetypal tale that knows no boundaries, as with Andrew Lam's evocation of *pho*, and the smells and tastes of ancient and modern Vietnam. The sensate memory traverses nations and generations to embolden the weary and delight the palates of new devotees. Yet as Britton Gildersleeve tells us in her palpable essay that calls up a colonial past of white-glove teas and streets that sing *Phàn dình Phùng* — "the war came."

Not surprisingly, in the next section, *War*, we witness the clear, the mysterious, and the elusive: the Vietnamese call it the "American War"; Americans call it the "Vietnamese War" — 1964-1975. Yet, as it has been pointed out, "The country is not the war; the war is not the country": 80 million people, the 14th most populous country in the world (half younger than 25); 50 ethnic groups each with its own language, in addition to the 87% majority Viet, and the Chinese Har and the French echoes of the colonial past. There is no possibility that this all-too-brief issue of *Nimrod* could encompass it. And yet, it seemed a timely challenge, as we in the United States again meet the many faces of aggression and guilt, and search for the spirit that binds us.

As we look at "War" thirty years later, groping through memory toward meaning, these writers reconstruct and re-vision strongly enough to enter our dreams with their poems, the stories that they tell, the stories that create us. Patrick Cole's "The Draft" shows us the nature of war, but it also presents a vigorous example of what it means to teach, to make it real, to make history not *abracadabra*. Wayne Karlin's "Eye of the Nation," with cinematographic economy, juxtaposes scenes from the war as experienced by soldiers on each side of the once impenetrable divide. And, as expected, there are poems of fathers gone and fathers returned unrecognizable; of mothers and wives inconsolable and ultimately looking ahead; of women carrying poles with bags of bread hanging from either end; of children making footprints that seem to move both forward and back. But expectation does not diminish the outcome, the immersion in a culture and time that are fading for some, that for others will exist for the first time.

And what *After* do we find that still speaks of that "sensory overload," that is Vietnam: the forests of dawn, the hot sun rising between hills and needle-clawed mangrove trees that bind water to the earth and promise life. Exposed, scavenged, and deforested, land and life, soil and souls become acid, parched deserts, cracked with nerves, split veins from shrimp farms, and soil salty as tears. But a spine of forested mountains connects the flat fertile deltas and the mouths of two rivers, the Red River in the north and the Mekong in the south. And all along the 900-mile length of Vietnam, that upside-down question mark, remains lush vegetation, acres of rice and melons and poetry carried on the wind and the winds of political change. For every tale of "dysfunction-junction," there is the heroic race on Honda Dream or Wave or Suzuki Viva, asserting independence, dangerously taunting fate and the torrential rains. And there is, as in the words of Vietnamese/American novelist Lan Cao, the bridge of language and literature that we build "to heal a mother's fear but also to repair generation after generation of past wrongs."

NOTE: Diacritical markings when Vietnamese is transliterated into the Roman alphabet are complex; there are differences of interpretation even among scholars and linguists. We have tried to reproduce as closely as possible the texts as our contributors have submitted them.

Anh Dao Kolbe, photograph

Tradition

John Balaban

Getting Beyond the War

Although it is commonplace now to say that "Vietnam is a country, not just the name of a war," discovering this has been slow for many of us. For anyone of the generation that grew up while the war was still going on, it was the war of course that led us to whatever appreciation we had of Vietnam as a culture with far greater depth and antiquity than we might have witnessed in our ten bloody years of military encounter. Soldiers—especially combat soldiers—often talked of the overwhelming beauty of the country. But few, remembering their intriguing glimpses of natural beauty, ever had the opportunity to discover what the Vietnamese themselves had thought of that familiar beauty in the several thousand years of their cultural identity. Few of us, including almost every reporter who ever went to Vietnam, could actually speak or read the language, much less its poetry, and it is in the poetry of Vietnam that its greatest monuments have been raised. Vietnam is a wet-rice agricultural civilization thousands of years old, but its cities and palaces and great villas were of wood and not much other than exquisite remnants has survived the annual monsoons. Poetry, that fragile construct, is Vietnam's enduring monument. As Ho Xuân Huong wrote 200 years ago:

Country Scene

The waterfall plunges in mist.
Who can describe this desolate scene:

the long white river sliding through
the emerald shadows of the ancient canopy

. . .a shepherd's horn echoing in the valley,
fish nets stretched to dry on sandy flats.

A bell is tolling, fading, fading
just like love. Only poetry lasts.

During the war, I volunteered as a civilian conscientious objector and worked as the field representative for a private agency that treated the most severely wounded children. The children that we brought to U.S. hospitals were riddled by bullets, slashed by cluster bomb flechettes, blinded and deafened by tossed grenades, had their lips and jaws shot away, their spines severed. One teen-aged girl was scalped by boat-propeller blades during a mortar attack on the river; others had their limbs blown off; one boy had his chin glued to his chest by napalm; one girl had her eyelids burned off by a white phosphorus artillery shell. One gun-shot toddler survived the massacre of her family in a pit because she was protected by their riddled bodies. The memory of such suffering would have been my sole, unadulterated sense of Vietnam had not my job often taken me into the countryside to talk to parents to explain what we could possibly do for their children at hospitals in the United States. My work afforded me a glimpse of another, more enduring Vietnam. This glimpse came on snatches of song through chance encounters with the sung poetry of the countryside.

Of course, at first, I had no clue as to what I was hearing. First, I encountered the sung poetry known as *vong co*, "lament for things past," epical poems of lost kings, doomed dynasties, and beautiful princesses. I would be waiting at a Mekong crossing for the ferry to come back, and I'd see a group of farmers back from market, huddled under the palms, gathered about a blind singer seated on the smooth earth tamped by bare and sandaled feet, a singer with a white wispy beard who was playing a 6-string steel guitar, accompanied by a blind woman, perhaps his wife, who kept rhythm with one foot on a wooden clapper, both of them attended by a sighted boy who watched the crowd and passed the hat. The steel strings had a bluesy quality as the singer bent his notes and his voice filled the riverbank with sadness. I wondered what it was all about. And then, back in Saigon at the zoo and botanical gardens, I saw another bedraggled blind pair, this time not playing a steel guitar, but rather the more traditional single-string viol, and I persuaded them to come to my apartment so I could record them. My education in sung poetry began that day, to the dismay of my landlady, who did not let such people into her house. *Di mot ngay dàng, hoc mot sàng khôn*. "Go out one day," the proverb says, "and come back with a basket full of wisdom."

Other times, I would be standing by a river as a little skiff motored by and I would hear a bit of song float past me, sometimes without ever even seeing the singer's face under the conical leaf hat, from where the song emerged to disappear in the wave wash on the bank and the stutter of the boat's two-cycle engine. Sometimes, I would catch the sunlight coming through the bamboo leaves of such a hat and I'd glimpse a couple of lines of poetry written in the old calligraphy known as chu Nôm. *Peasants with poetry sewn into their hats?* Vietnam was always widening its mystery. Sometimes, I would be waiting in an orchard behind a family's house as they all came to a decision about sending their injured child to America in our care and, off in the distance, lost in the bananas and papaya, a woman's voice would start up in song…usually a lone voice because, except for the blind *vong co* singers, most of what I heard was *ca dao*: brief lyric poems in a tradition at least 1000 years old, passed down by song and polished by each new singer who wished to make a change.[1] The sung poetry of *ca dao* seemed to belong to the most ordinary of country people.

In 1971-72, after my alternative service was over and I had returned to start a teaching career at Penn State, I received a Younger Humanist Fellowship from the National Endowment for the Humanities and so, while the war was still nattering on, I returned to Vietnam to spend a year recording *ca dao*. My plan was simple: walking up to farmers and fishermen and women working old Singer pedal sewing machines, I asked them to sing their favorite poems into my tape recorder.[2] I must have seemed very peculiar if not exactly threatening: a lone American, not wearing a uniform, out there in the war zone with my bookbag and tape recorder. I am still amazed that these country people even talked to me, much less agreed to sing poetry into my recorder. But *ca dao* belongs so naturally to the people who create it that perhaps it seemed to them not the least surprising that a foreigner would also want to know about it. In that whole year of recording, I never encountered anyone who did not know some *ca dao*. The ubiquity of the poetry (and the concordant tradition of proverbs known as *tuc ngu*) speaks to how much the oral folk poetry has served as a millennial record of Vietnamese aspiration, feeling, and belief. I recorded some five hundred poems that year from about thirty singers from the Mekong Delta, the Central Highlands, and the old capital of Hue. Over the decades since those collecting forays into the war-torn countryside, I have often thought what might have been the parallel luck of a young Vietnamese with a tape-recorder walking up to American farmhouses with the same request.

To have a sense of this poetry and what these unlettered farmers were holding in their heads, one has to understand word tone, something that does not occur in English. But in Vietnamese every syllable has a pitch or tone (indicated in writing by the diacritical marks over or under vowels in the modern roman script). Depending on the regional dialect, there are either six or five pitches possible. Each of them changes the meaning of the syllable, for instance:

la: to shout (high level tone)
là: to be (falling tone)
lả: tired (falling-rising tone)
lã: insipid (high-constricted, broken tone)
lá: leaf (high-rising tone)
lạ: strange (low-constricted tone).

Hoi   cô   tát   n_uoc   bên   dàng.
Oh,   girl bailing water   by   roadside,

Sao   cô   múc   ánh   trang   vàng   do di?
Why (girl) ladle light moon   gold pour out?

(Oh, girl, bailing water by the roadside,
why pour off the moon's golden light?)

While tones fall at random in speech or in prose, in poetry the tones are regulated to fall at certain feet in the prosodic line. Once you have an arrangement of linguistic word pitch it is not a big step to musical pitch. This is where the melodies of *ca ðao* begin. It is the melodies of *ca ðao* that animate the repertoires of the singers.[3]

Here are some of the "rules" for the above *Lục Bát* (6/8-syllable) couplet: The second, sixth, and eighth syllables of each line must be "even" tones (la or là, in the above) whereas the fourth syllables must be any one of the other tones, which are all considered "sharp." Rhymes properly fall only on words that have "even" tones, but these words should not be the *same* even tone. In the couplet above, the sixth and final syllable of the first line

4

(*đàng*) rhymes with the sixth syllable of the next line (*vàng*). The eighth syllable of the second line (*đi*) is a potential new rhyme that the singer could use to start linking in any number of additional couplets, folding in new rhymes each time. All this is retained in the oral poet's ear. While it might seem a complex construct for composers who often do not read or write, the six-eight couplet is only one of several prosodic forms available, although perhaps the most common for the past two hundred years or so.

Poetry in Vietnam flows from two great sources. The folk poetry is probably as old as the Vietnamese themselves and may have origins as distant as the Mon-Khmer traditions from which the Vietnamese language emerged thousands of years ago.[4] The other great source of poetry is more recent: the *literary* tradition which entered Vietnam with the Chinese conquest 2000 years ago, reaching its most enduring influence in the regulated verse form (*lu-shih*) of the 8th century C.E. Like the Italian sonnet in the West, but more compressed in form, the *lu-shih* became the vehicle for sophisticated lyric expression in languages as diverse as Tibetan, Korean, Japanese, and Vietnamese. Syntactic similarities between Chinese and Vietnamese made the form a natural acquisition for the Vietnamese even before they threw out the Chinese invaders in 939 C.E. And when the newly independent Vietnamese court fashioned itself on the Chinese imperial model, the form became the intellectual index for anyone hoping to enter the civil service and polite society. As a vehicle for "what is on the mind intently," it had lyrical use in Vietnam into the 1930s with its last great practitioner, the poet and journalist Tan Dà.

Here is a regulated verse of Ho Xuân Huong, the aristocratic concubine of the early 1800s who often employed the ancient form with subversive intent by concealing a complete *double entendre* within the apparent landscape, but nonetheless observing all the traditional rules of an eight-line poem, with seven syllables per line, with rhymes at the end of the 1st, 2nd, 4th, 6th, and 8th lines, and with parallel syntactic structure in the middle four lines:

Dèo Ba Dôi

Môt dèo, môt dèo, lai môt dèo,
Khen ai khéo tac canh cheo leo.
Cua son do loét tùm hum nóc,
Hòn dá xanh rì lún phún rêu.
Lat leo cành thông con gió thoc,
Dam dìa lá lieu giot suong gieo.
Hien nhân, quân tu ai mà chang. . .
Moi goi, chon chân van muon trèo.

Three Mountain Pass

A cliff face. Another. And still a third.
Who was so skilled to carve this craggy scene

the cavern's red door, the ridge's narrow cleft,
the black knoll bearded with little mosses?

A twisting pine bough plunges in the wind,
showering a willow's leaves with glistening drops.

Gentlemen, lords, who could refuse, though weary
and shaky in his knees, to mount once more?[5]

By the 19th century, Vietnamese scholars and royalty were composing palindromes in the form, sometimes in two languages at once, as in one poem that, when one comes to its last word and starts reading backwards, shifts languages from Vietnamese to a *lu-shih* in Chinese. The late French mathematician Pierre Daudin, researching palindromes written for such "intellectual recreation," discovered the circular ("anacyclique") palindrome below composed by the Emperor Thieu-Tri (1841-1847) and set in jade inlay in a wooden panel at the Long-An Palace.[6] It is nothing less than twelve perfect *lu-shih* that can be unlocked, each with differing meaning, depending on whatever ray one starts with, going left to right, right to left, inside out, or outside in. It fairly defies Western imagination.

These two great streams of poetry—the oral and the literary—often run together and mix, enriching the great flow of Vietnamese poetry over the centuries. Part of the pleasure in reading Ho Xuân Huong, for example, is finding in her *lu-shih* verse (with its ancient and noble pedigree) a vocabulary from the street or marketplace. Nguyen Du (1765-1820), her famous contemporary, took the *Luc Bát* couplet from the folk poetry and, using its possibility of rhyme linkage, fashioned his great classical poem, *The Tale of Kieu*, in 3254 lines of *ca dao* couplets, while borrowing his narrative from a Chinese novel. At its best, the literary poetry was always in touch with the folk tradition, so much so that it is not unusual even today to encounter ordinary Vietnamese who can recite the entire *Tale of Kieu* from memory. Even in the best fiction writing of modern Vietnam, say, in the short stories of Nguyen Huy Thiêp, one can find the imagistic power and simple word stock of *ca dao*, while at the same time encountering the complexities of suggestion favored by the 19th-Century court with its palindromes for "intellectual recreation."

It is hard for Westerners to fathom a culture where poetry figures so prominently, not just in the lives of the educated, but in the lives of farmers as well. In Vietnam you can court with poetry (the *ca dao* at the beginning of this little survey is a young man's attempt at getting the girl's attention). You can gamble on poetry. Political debates can be won with a poem ("there's a poem to prove it, too!"). Once, to my amazement, I stopped a street fight that was brewing with some cyclo drivers by quoting the proverb: "The wise man shuts his mouth; the strong man folds his arms." For these sorts of things to happen around poetry, poetry must go pretty deeply into the culture.

Indeed, poetry in Vietnam has often seemed to have greater-than-human power. In 1076 C.E., Marshall Ly Thuong Kiet (1019-1105) ordered the following poem painted in honey on the leaves of banana trees as he gathered his forces to drive out the Chinese.

> The southern mountains are the Southern Ruler's.
> This is written in the Celestial Book.
> Those who try to conquer this land
> Will surely suffer defeat.

南 國 山 河 南 帝 居

截 然 定 分 在 天 書

如 何 逆 虜 來 侵 犯

汝 等 行 看 取 敗 虛

When his troops found the poems, with the characters now eaten by ants that had followed the honey strokes, it seemed to them clearly an expression of divine will and heavenly mandate. They rallied and won the battle. Or so the legend says.

Beside its power to persuade, to entertain, and to express both personal and divine truths, poetry can also be a test of another's character. This is true even today for government officials for whom, one would imagine, the old poetry would be a thing of the feudal past. During the height of the Cold War, in the mid-1980s, along with the poets Denise Levertov, Roland Flint, and William Meredith, then the Poet to the Library of Congress, I was invited to an international meeting of writers in Sofia, Bulgaria. Along with the American poets, there were fiction writers, including Erskine Caldwell, John Cheever, and William Gaddis. And along with the Americans, there were writers from everywhere on the planet, from Iceland to Vietnam. The Bulgarian Writers Union put up about 400 of us at their government's expense at the Hotel Parc Moskva. It must have cost them a fortune to feed this artistic battalion, providing us with plane tickets and city tours, and giving each one of us a packet with the equivalent of about one hundred dollars in *leva* in spending money.

It was the first time I had met *North* Vietnamese. I was curious about them and had given one of their delegation poets a copy of my first translations of *ca ∂ao*. They were curious about me. How come this American spoke Vietnamese in the southern dialect? Where did he learn it? Why? Finally, one afternoon about eight of them just sat me down in the hotel lobby and started firing questions. It had been more than a decade since I had spoken Vietnamese and I could hardly understand them. "That's okay," one said in French. "Do you know French?"

I knew a little French. So they began again asking me in French about what I had done in Vietnam. It was rapid-fire questioning from several people at once and it was bewildering. I flushed when I realized I was being interrogated, albeit in the main lobby. When I tried to explain my alternative service to the military, it seemed I just couldn't make myself clear enough. My answers weren't complete, weren't satisfying. I realized if I got up to go, it would just confirm their probable suspicions that I was a CIA agent sent to spy on them. Now they were slipping some English into the flow of Vietnamese and French.

Finally, the one who seemed to be in charge motioned for the others to stop. He had my first edition of *Ca Dao Vietnam* in his hand and he began to flip through the poems and translations. He stopped on the last poem in the book:

At the Exiled King's River Pavilion

Evening, and all around the King's pavilion
people are sitting, fishing, sad and grieving,
loving, in love, remembering, waiting, watching.
Whose boat plies the river mists
offering so many river songs
to move these mountains and rivers, our nation?

"Who wrote this poem, Professor Balaban?" he asked and smiled.

I smiled back. I could see where this was going. "As you know," I said, "*ca ∂ao* are not written. They are oral, passed down by song."

His smile faded.

"...but this one," I added, "is unusual. It has a line in it from the *The Tale of Kieu* and refers to the disappearance of young King

9

Duy Tân…"

"Yes, yes," he said, "who *wrote* it?"

"Thúc Gia Thi, pen name: 'Ung Bình.'"

Now everyone was smiling. Only a real translator could know a detail like that. I had been vetted through poetry.

Today, that awkward if interesting encounter of nearly twenty years ago seems a world away. Diplomatic relations between the U.S. and Vietnam are now restored. Hanoi is filled with American backpackers, while its swankier hotels compare with any in the world. More than half of the Vietnamese alive today were born after the war and a new generation of young Americans who learned quite good Vietnamese in college are taking on new translations. What awaits them is a startling bright range of contemporary fiction writing, thousands of folk poems that have never been recorded, and centuries of poetry, some of it in the old script called chu Nôm, including the regulated verse of the great statesman and humanist Nguyen Trãi, and the untranslated Zen poetry of the Buddhist "father-mother" kings of the Ly and Tran dynasties (1009-1413). A lot of the poetry, including the *ca dao* oral poetry, has been preserved in handwritten or woodblock manuscripts in chu Nôm and remains untransliterated into modern Vietnamese, let alone translated into English.[7] Along with poetry there are vast Nôm manuscript holdings in medicine, religion, philosophy, drama, music, and history and not just in Vietnam, but in national libraries through-out the world: in France, the Vatican, Madrid, Lisbon, Holland, China, Japan, the United States, and England.

The war, which caused pain and anguish for millions, was nonetheless only a part of the story.

---

[1] *Ca dao* (pronounced "ka zow" or "ka yow") is a term borrowed from the Chinese "Ko Yaom," "song and ballads." Much of Vietnamese literary terminology has been borrowed from Chinese in the way that English has borrowed from, say, Classical Greek or Renaissance Italian. *Ca dao* themselves are purely Vietnamese in origin.

[2] Readers may be interested in hearing some of the original record-ings at www.johnbalaban.com . For a fuller discussion see my *Ca Dao Việt Nam: Vietnamese Folk Poetry* (Copper Canyon, 2003).

[3] Not melody in the contemporary Western sense, but rather "cantillations" or "singing without song." Solange Corbin, "La Cantillation des rituels chrétiens," *Revue de Musicologie*. Vol. XLVII. July, 1961, pp. 3-36. For application to Vietnamese music, see Tran Van Khê, "Musique Bouddhique Au Viet-Nam," in Jacques Porte, *Encyclopédie des Musiques Sacrées*. (Paris: Labergerie, 1968), Vol.1, pp. 222-240.

[4] See David Thomas and Robert K. Headley, Jr., "More on Mon-Khmer Subgroupings," *Lingua* 25 (1970), p. 404. And also: Roger Legay and K'Mloi Da Got, "Prières Lac Accompagnant Les Rites Agraires," *Bulletin de la Société des Études Indochinoises*, Tome XLVI, No.2. 2e Trimestre, 1971, p. 186.

[5] The late scholar Maurice Durand notes (*L'Oeuvre de la poétesse vietnamienne Ho Xuân Huong* [Paris: Adrien-Maisonneuve, 1968], p. 13) that this range is almost certainly the Dèo Tam-Diêp in central North Vietnam where the mountains are calcareous and of a blackish color but, he adds innocently, "l'on n'a pas de grotte avec une grande ouverture." Pines are traditionally male; willows, female.

[6] Pierre Daudin, "Poèmes anacycliques de l'Empereur Thieu-Tri," *Bulletin de la Société des Études Indochinoises* 47, no. 1(1972): pp. 2-24, 49, no.2 (1974): pp. 226-51. See his articles for a French translation.

[7] More about chi Nôm can be found at www.nomfoundation.org .

Anh Dao Kolbe, "Hanoi Tea Seller," photo

A Tiny Bird

A tiny bird with red feathers,
a tiny bird with black beak
drinks up the lotus pond day by day.
Perhaps I must leave you.

The Outpost Soldier

Here are only cliffs and crags,
bird tracks, beasts shuffling, locusts chirring,
and jungle trees rustling their music.
A bird calls out from a gnarled tree.
I've lived in the forest for three years.

The Concubine

As second wife, I never liked the first,
who locks the door each night and climbs in bed
while I sleep on a mat outside.
At dawn she calls out, "Hey, Two, get up.
Slice potatoes and pound the beans."
Potatoes. Beans. Because my parents were poor.

*Translated from the Vietnamese
by John Balaban*

*Reprinted from Ca Dao Viêt Nam: Vietnamese Folk Poetry, *Copper Canyon Press, 2003.*

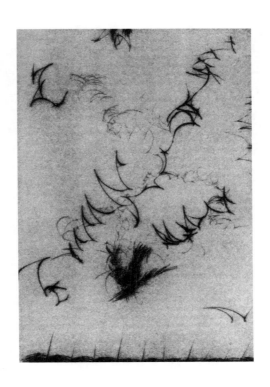

Thân em lấy lẽ chả hề,
Có như chính thất mà lê giữa giường,
Tối tối chị giữ mất buồng,
Cho em manh chiếu, nằm suông nhà ngoài,
Sáng sáng chị gọi: Ở hai!
Bấy giờ trở dậy, thái khoai đâm bèo,
Vì chưng bác mẹ tôi nghèo,
Cho nên tôi phải đâm bèo, thái khoai.

The Concubine

*Francisco Toledo, drypoint etching from limited edition portfolio, *Trece Maneras de Mirar un Mirlo,* 1981.

Lê Phạm Lê

Simplicity

Exiled in this strange land
we build our tent-site on sand,

rocks soft to our work-hardened hands.
At night when the moon shines

we recite poems. The hammock sways.
A mother's song lures her child to peace.

Beyond the monkey-bridge,
a boat rocks the waves.

Wind, carry my worries
to the other side of the sea!

Midnight

In my hazy dream you appear
and disappear, father,

and I am young again, waiting at the gate
for you to pick me up from school

in Dalat, hometown, city of misty rain.

In Pulau Bidong Refugee Camp

After days adrift our boat beached
on a strange land that stormy night,
our country a distant dream
in the fading light,

a refugee camp our asylum
on the deserted island,
a blue tarp open to rain, open to wind
kidding the wanderers too long.

Far from camp
on the wet mountainside
we cut leaves to make walls
for our pain. . . .

Dáng Yêu by Lê Phạm Lê

Tôi nhớ thật nhiều
Chiếc cầu nhỏ xinh xinh
Nằm vắt ngang giữa hai ngôi biệt thự,
Nơi đó mình chia tay nhau
Vào một buổi chiều gió lạnh đầu đông
Mưa bay lất phất.
Tôi cố ngăn dòng nước mắt,
Và khuôn mặt người đượm buồn xa xăm.

Thế rồi tôi đã ra đi,
Bỏ lại sau lưng
Con đường mòn từ từ mất hút,
Và lũ kỷ niệm khó quên.

Từ ấy đã lâu.
Thời gian vẫn biền biệt trôi qua,
Không gian muôn trùng cách xa.
Cuộc sống có bao nhiêu biên giới
Mà con người không thể vượt qua?
Có lần người đến thăm tôi
Và dòng đời vẫn trôi...

Bỗng dưng hôm nay
Tôi trở lại nơi nầy,
Bâng khuâng, ngỡ ngàng
Dù cảnh cũ không mấy đổi thay.
Bây giờ là mùa xuân,
Hoa bên thềm nở rộ.
Chiếc cầu nhỏ thân thương ngày xưa vẫn còn đó,
Nhưng người đã đi thật xa.
Có chọn lựa nào không mất mát, xót xa?

Shape of Love

How I miss the small bridge
between the two buildings
where we said goodbye
that evening at winter's beginning —
slap of rain,
tears I tried to hold back,
a melancholy look on your face.

I am already gone,
leaving behind a path
gradually disappearing.

Now across time,
across distances we cannot cross,
still you come to me
and life goes on.

But is there ever choice
without loss?
I return to the old scene
almost unchanged:

springtime, cherries blossoming
along the walk,
the old bridge still standing,
only you no longer here.

*Translated from the Vietnamese
by Nancy Arbuthnot and Lê Phạm Lê*

PHAM DUY KHIEM

The Mountain of Waiting

Just before arriving at Lang Don, the traveler who climbs from the delta towards the High Country will notice, to the right of the old Tonkinese road, a small isolated mountain. At the summit, a rock rises up which suggests the shape of a woman standing with a child in her arms; the similarity becomes especially striking towards evening, as the sun approaches the horizon.

This is "Nui Vong-Phu," the "Mountain of the woman who waits for her husband." And this is the story that is told about it.

❊ ❊ ❊

Long ago, in a village in the high country, there lived two orphans, a young man of twenty, and his sister, who was no older than seven. Alone in the world, they were everything to each other.

One day a passing Chinese astrologer, who was consulted by the young man about their future, told him, "If such were the days and times of your births, you will inevitably marry your sister. Nothing can change the path of destiny."

The terrible prediction appalled the young man; it haunted him day and night. Finally, in a state of panic, he made an extreme decision.

One day when he was going to cut wood in the forest, he took his sister with him. Taking advantage of a moment when she had her back turned towards him, he knocked her down with a blow from his axe and ran away.

He was delivered from his obsession, but for some time the horror of his crime pursued him. He changed his name, gradually became calm again little by little, and finally established himself at Lang Son.

Many years passed. He married the daughter of a merchant. She gave him a son and made him very happy.

❋ ❋ ❋

One day, on entering the inner courtyard of their home, he found his wife busy drying her long black hair, as she sat in the bright sunlight. She had her back turned to him and had not seen him enter. At the moment when she slid the comb through her smooth black hair which she had raised with her other hand, he discovered, below the nape of her neck, a long scar.

He asked her the origin of the scar. After having hesitated slightly, she wept as she told him her story: "I am not the real daughter of the man whom I call my father, but only his adopted daughter.

"As an orphan, I lived with my older brother, who was all the family I had. Fifteen years ago, he wounded me with a blow from his axe and abandoned me in the forest. I was saved by robbers. Shortly afterwards, when they were about to be captured, they suddenly ran away from their den, and I was found there. A merchant, who had just lost his own daughter, had pity on me and took me in . . . .

"I do not know what happened to my brother and I was never able to explain his action to myself . . . .We loved each other very much."

The face of the young woman was bathed in tears. The man controlled his emotions, and asked her to tell him the precise name of her father and that of the village where she was born.

When there was no more possibility of doubt, he succeeded in keeping the appalling secret to himself. But he was ashamed and horrified by what he had done and felt incapable of continuing their life together. He invented a pretext to leave her.

❋ ❋ ❋

During the six months which his voyage should have taken, his wife waited for him, patient and resigned. But the time appointed for his return had passed long ago and she was always alone with her son.

Each evening she took the child in her arms and climbed the mountain, in order to scan the distance for the return of her absent husband. When she reached the summit of the mountain, she would stand there, her eyes fixed on the horizon.

She was changed into stone, and it is in this form that one can still see her, upright against the sky, motionless in her eternal waiting.

※ ※ ※

Many Vietnamese poets have been inspired to write poems about the legendary Mountain. Here is one of them, as far as it can be conveyed in a translation:

Day after day, month after month, year after year . . .waiting
—In the sun, in the night, with the wind, under the rain
This heart of hard gold and of faithful stone.

Translated from the French by Harry Aveling

Anh Dao Kolbe, "Vinh Long Rice Crackle," photograph

ANDREW LAM

Star Anise, Charred Onion, and Five Kinds of Basil

A bright Saigon morning in March, 1975. At Mrs. Tran's restaurant on Pasteur Street bad news came blaring on the radio. Da Nang was under attack. Two Russian MIGs had flown all the way from Hanoi to the central highlands without ARVN resistance. Bombarded by VC mortar, the city was veiled in black smoke.

Everyone—customers, waiters, a dozen passers-by, even Mrs. Tran's mangy, flea-bitten German shepherd—all held their breath and listened. The plump and sturdy matron, too, stayed her cleaver on the large chopping block where she'd been slicing beef tripe. With closed eyes she listened. Her husband, a captain in the Marines, was stationed north of Da Nang. Since mid-February she had no news of him.

Customers broke out in gossip when the special news report ended, some openly wept over their uneaten soup, others, their faces ashen, pushed their chairs and stood up and left without paying. Mrs. Tran didn't care. She began to remove her jade bracelet, gold Buddha necklace and two ruby earrings, then wrapped them in a white handkerchief. She handed the tiny bundle to her daughter, Nga, the dreamy-eyed teenager who was busy staring at the bright street outside, where flame trees bloomed red and orange, and where people rushed here and there in a state of panic.

"Stop daydreaming, my child," Mrs. Tran scolded her, "put this away and write this down. Get pen and paper. You should have memorized it by now, the way you devour poetry, but I know you haven't. And may Lady Buddha Quan Yin protect us all."

Allow the oxtail and marrow bones to unleash their flavor, and the star anise and cloves to permeate thoroughly, making it a worthy base for the delicate rice noodles, which are, as you know, freshly cooked for each bowl.

In 1964, in the middle of the monsoon season, 50 South Vietnamese soldiers with northern accents and ancestry, in a program concocted by the CIA, parachuted back into northern territories to act as spies. Of the 50, Mr. Chi Nguyen was the only one who managed to elude capture and to blend in with the general populace.

Now in Sacramento, California, a wizened old man with a toothless grin and a throaty voice, Mr. Nguyen told his story to a pot-bellied reporter from the *Sacramento Bee*. Having infiltrated Hanoi, he ordered *pho* in a wellknown restaurant near Hoan Kiem Lake. In the middle of eating his soup he spotted Vu, his best friend and comrade in espionage, sitting at another table. They made eye contact but did not dare talk. Mr. Nguyen desperately wanted to warn Vu to stop slurping so loudly, as he was attracting attention. But before he could gesture or say a word, Vu already made a second mistake, which proved fatal: He ordered a second bowl.

Customers and waiters gasped. Heads turned. For it was a time of ration and of self-sacrifice, a time of anti-bourgeois behaviors, and no one, not even Uncle Ho himself, especially him, ever ordered a second bowl. Eat a second bowl and you'd have committed an anti-revolutionary act. Eat too much and you'd have shown your true bourgeois colors. Eat more than your share and you'd never survive the communist paradise.

Vu never did. Like the others from the group, he was promptly arrested, tortured, then, four months later, executed on espionage charges. Mr. Nguyen himself survived by sheer luck: he had a small stomach and, besides, had never forgotten the unforgiving nature of the north.

After the war ended he left the country on a boat with his wife and children. The wife, a peasant, did not know that he was a spy for the South until they reached the United States. The children, too busy becoming Americans, didn't care. But it was not his story of espionage that Mr. Nguyen recalled now with fondness. It was his first bowl of soup in Hanoi. "You know what," he said to the reporter in a voice now tinged with longing, "it was the best bowl of *pho* I ever had. Simple, but delicious. No garnish, just a squeeze of lime on a few pieces of raw beef the size of your fingernail, and the broth—oh la la, it smelled distinctly of star anise and charred onion."

"I was hungry with my eyes and nose even if my stomach couldn't hold," said Mr. Nguyen. "If I could have eaten like Vu, poor bastard, I probably would have, at the risk of death and destruction, ordered another bowl." Then at the thought of his own death and destruction the old man fell into a laughing fit that almost killed him, his eyes, tearing, disappeared under wrinkling epicanthic folds.

Mr. Nguyen grew five kinds of basil all in his garden in Sacramento, plus a few other herbs, like Vietnamese coriander, lemongrass, mint, and many bushes of star anise flowers and some parsnip. "So where is home now for you, Mr. Nguyen?" asked the *Bee* reporter. Home, he said, is his pungent garden, home is the hot summer breeze in which herbal aromas waft and fold. Home is what you run away from in your youth, only to be trapped again in longing for it in your old age. Faraway restaurants are known to order his anise and coriander. "Smell this," he said as he mashed a dark green basil leaf between his tobacco-stained fingers and held its fragrant juice against the reporter's nose. "Smell good, yes, yes? This smell, it makes me remember, it takes me all the way back."

To make pho *be of many minds. The side dishes alone can distract you from the main broth. The broth demands constant care, for without it, my dear, you have nothing.*

Late afternoon of the last day of April in 1975, the sun burned like a piece of coal overhead, an eerie silence reigned over the entire city, and communist tanks crashed through the gilded gates of an empty Independence Palace. Inside, a fat president named Big Minh, who had been president for a day, sat waiting to surrender. The city had fallen, and young Viet-Congs sat on rusty mud-caked trucks and tanks with awe and bewilderment on their sunburnt faces. Saigon was beautiful, rich beyond their imagination, not the poor, wretched place suffering under imperial powers their leaders had filled their heads with all those years in the jungle. Already some began to ponder that question that is still argued to this day: who's liberating whom?

From behind curtains and over red and purple bougainvillea-veiled walls, or hidden behind tamarind and flame trees, well-fed, discreet Saigonese stole glimpses at their emaciated conquerors, though a few of their rowdier children climbed the walls, and, thinking it was yet another military parade, hollered and waved.

At the dock, it was another story. Thousands had gathered and were jostling each other onto the planks of waiting ships. Nga herself boarded a crowded boat with her younger brother. Their aunt was with them. Nga's mother had accompanied the three to the dock but decided to stay and wait for news of her husband. Her aged parents, besides, needed her back in Quang Ngai province, if they'd survived. Even if they hadn't, she needed to fulfill her filial duties and bury them properly. With hoarse, weeping voices, Nga, her little brother, and their young aunt all begged Mrs. Tran to come along—"Please, sister, I beg you, think of the children!"; "Oh mother, how can you possibly not come?"; "Ma, I'm so scared!" But Mrs. Tran was adamant. "Go! Go with my blessing. And you, take care of my children like your own," she ordered her younger sister, and hastily stuffed all the gold and dollars she had traded earlier that morning into her sister's and daughter's outreached hands. She imagined herself giving away dowry at her daughter's wedding, which she, in flash of prescience, saw as taking place on a kept lawn and beside a lake dotted with sailboats. She even saw the groom's face, a smiling, blue-eyed stranger who was now lifting her daughter's pearl-studded veil to kiss her.

The ship engine rumbled, the smell of diesel assaulted the air, her children called out desperately for their mother, but Mrs. Tran kept walking. She willed herself not to look back, not even once. On the streets and sidewalks near the dock, motorbikes and cars and army jeeps and suitcases and clothes were left abandoned. And in the air Vietnamese *dong*—green, red, and orange—fluttered like butterflies. This colorful South Vietnamese currency had lost all its value that morning and was now worth only as much as the paper mock offerings one burned for the dead. However, the street urchins did not know this. A band of them, wearing new clothes that were too big for them, were amassing the notes they had coveted for so long, singing gleefully their prophetic ditty of what was to come, "Oh we're paupers who turned into princes and kings, and we'll run the world with our ding-a-lings."

In the dying light of April, Mrs. Tran mumbled her Buddhist prayers while clutching her rosary made of black bodhi seeds, which were shiny from years of use. She kept on walking. Behind her one ship after another left the harbor.

A bowl of pho *with marrow served on the side is treasure. A dish of oxtail bone to accompany it, sprinkled with green onion, black pepper and freshly chopped chili, is love.*

A windy autumn morning in the mid-1960s, the sky a be-
nevolent blue, the war undecided, a handsome young man named
Quang set sail. Long before leaving was thought possible, before
the word *vuot-bien*—to cross the border—was to become a household word, Quang alone had already seen the seven seas. A genius
with pipes and propellers, a doctor of ailing engines, he could hear
their unquiet murmurs and name their ailments without fail. He
would then set out to fix them and made himself indispensable to
the Golden Seahorse shipping line from Hong Kong, who paid a
small fortune to the foreign department in Saigon to purchase his
exit visa and, in doing so, gave him the world.

The night before he left, his mother, pricking her thigh with a
small hairpin under the table so that she wouldn't have to pay
attention to the real pain of losing her only son, said in a stem
voice: "Go! Please go! I'd rather have you alive in Morocco than
coming back to me in a body bag from the DMZ. Go! Save
yourself. And listen to me, unless there is real peace, don't you dare
come back."

So, there was a war and he was sailing far away from it.
There was a war and he didn't sleep well in any port or on any
ocean. Têt offensive and he was in Madagascar. His mother's death
and he wept all the way to Iceland. His best friend mortally
wounded in Dalak and he watched a gorgeous sunset from Sydney
with a Chivas Regal bottle as his companion.

When the war ended and the communists won, he couldn't
come home. He kept his promise to his mother and kept going,
though Quang kept dreaming of his homeland and everyone he
knew there. His yearning over time made him at once handsome
yet impossibly aloof. He had no friends and his lovers were fleeting
and far between. Always, he dreamed of his mother's house, his
little hamlet on the outskirts of Saigon by the river, and, of course,
his sweetheart who had long ago married and was already a
mother of three. In dreams, in reveries, Quang stepped off his ship
with gifts in hand and shouted out to all the people he knew and
loved, but, in reality, the gifts, bought and wrapped, stayed locked
in his cabinet, and, since there was no real peace, he never returned.

On a beach in Reunion one day, a lush green island with
waterfalls and gentle luring waves, though he was already late and
should have been heading back to his ship, Quang kept on walking. Far down the beach, Quang saw a little makeshift restaurant

with coconut trees and thatched roof and, though he really should have been getting back, he headed for it. A dark-skinned, elegant-looking mademoiselle greeted him with a bright smile and gave him the menu. Conch and fish he had plenty but as Quang scanned the menu with the boredom of someone who had eaten too many exotic meals, he saw at the bottom of the page a word that caused him to sit up and stare: "Fo."

Remember, you have to learn to be patient. It takes cooking all night for a broth to be ready in the morning. Skim the surface for scum that boiled to the top, make sure the broth is perfectly clear, yet its taste should linger.

Dawn in her memories: she stretches like a kitten on her bed next to the large French window on the second floor. It looks out to other balconies, eight houses in all that share a leafy and mildewed courtyard. She hears the solemn sounds of Buddhist chanting from Old Lady Muoi who lives across the way. In her memories the wind is always cool and supple, and her curtains sway just so, and the smell of sandalwood incense, fragrant and holy, along with her mother's complex aromatic broth from the restaurant downstairs, would fill her nostrils.

On the balcony to the right Toan, a boy her age, is already up, diligently practicing his martial arts. She can hear the dull, thudding sounds from the impact his feet and fists make against the sandbag that hangs from the eave of his roof. If she peeks, she can see the beads of sweat on his bare shoulders, his stomach rippling with abdominal muscles in the early light. Sometimes their eyes meet for half a second, and it is enough for the boy to be completely disarmed. He turns as red as a firecracker and the sandbag suffers more assaults than usual, and she hides behind the curtain, her hand on her mouth to stifle a giggle.

Other times, Nga remembers this: wild parrots squabbling over the ripened fruits on the single mangosteen tree in the middle of the courtyard, and Mai, the servant next door, singing a song from her favorite Cai Luong opera while doing the laundry, her voice sad and mournful; the heat rising.

Downstairs, in the restaurant kitchen, her mother, who had risen hours before dawn, is already preparing the day's fare with the help of her two servants. Soon the noise of the wooden chairs being dragged on the tile floor, of chatting customers, of motorcycle mufflers, of children on their way to school, will rule the world. But not now. Not yet. Now there is only a stillness in the salty dawn.

Nga will always associate this moment with home, a sweetness in the world so rare that it can now be had only in the recalling. She can feel it still, hear it perhaps with more clarity because of her unfulfilled longings, and the years. Her mother humming softly, ladles against the pots and pans, and the steady chopping sound of the cleaver on the worn wooden block, Old Lady Muoi's pious chanting, Toan's sandbag being pummeled, his roan back, and Mai's lovely and sad voice . . . .

All this—her unhurried lullaby, what insulates and owns her still, even now, from an unfathomable distance.

The bowl comes to you hot, extremely. That's how the aroma reaches the diner. Imagine dropping freshly cut onions into a bowl of cold soup—you will smell nothing, a waste of all the efforts.

A hot August day in San Jose at the turn of the millennium, Kevin Pham, a boyish 24-year-old electrical and computer engineer working for Hewlett Packard, entered "pho soup" in his favorite search engine. The number of hits that came back was staggering: 2883. Kevin wasn't sure exactly why he entered "pho." He could easily have entered "manga" or "kung fu movies" or a dozen other things that always lurked at the edge of his pop culture-flooded mind. But it was near lunch time, and as he later wrote to Bernard, his wealthy ex-dorm-mate from U.C. Berkeley now living in Brussels, "I suppose I was both hungry and missing my mom's cooking." It was a fateful choice. For then, almost as a joke, he began a website called *whatpho?.com*, a popular site that rated various *pho* restaurants in California and had 10,000 hits daily. Five bowls for the best. Two for mediocre ones, and bad ones, really bad ones, got a pair of broken chopsticks.

A few months after he built his site Bernard sent him a cryptic email:

Dearest K.,

If you want to eat the best *pho* in Europe come to Belgium. Your homeland's exquisite broth travels—to mine. Stay with me as long as you like and we can make many an excursion. Besides, I promised you "moules et frites." Just tell me when and I'll send tix.

Tu me manques,

Bernard

So Kevin came to Belgium on a culinary quest—and found himself driving up a country road one sunny afternoon with an enigmatic but beaming Bernard who intermittently stole glimpses at his profile as they drove, their black Porsche zooming down country lanes stirring up afternoon dust.

Soon they came to a small forest, then an impressive medieval castle that loomed over the hedges. "Are you sure, Bernard?" Kevin said. "It's private property."

"Just relax and enjoy the ride, would you, babe," Bernard said. "I have a surprise for you."

At the moat, standing on the drawbridge, Kevin stopped. And sniffed. He had expected it, but it still shocked him. It was unmistakable. There it was, that complex aroma wafting in the air—cinnamon and cloves and ginger and fish sauce and star anise and beef broth. Someone was making *pho*.

Bernard steered him down a dark staircase toward an enormous kitchen, the kind that could cater to 300 people. In the middle of it stood an elegant Asian woman in her mid-30s, two little mixed-race children, a boy of 4 and a girl of 7, playing on a slide next to her. At the far corner, a blond maid was skimming the soup. The Asian woman greeted Bernard with kisses and then she turned warmly and addressed Kevin in Vietnamese. "Here you are. I've been waiting for a long time. I thought you both got lost in the woods." Then she kissed him on both cheeks. "Bernard spoke so often about you that I started to miss you too."

The shank and oxtail bone, pick them carefully. Make sure there's plenty of marrow inside the shanks and, as for the oxtail, don't buy those that are too large, or they can't fit in the bowl for a side dish, and can often overwhelm the diner.

"Fo" was once *pho*, after many generations, so Quang found out on that beach in Reunion. Still, who would complain about spellings when the broth simmered in the kitchen? There was no rice noodle in what survived, no star anise smell, not even fish sauce. The mademoiselle with a slender figure and a bright smile made noodle out of tapioca. She rubbed it into uneven strings between her dexterous fingers, then boiled it.

Yet it was "*un plat Vietnamien*," as she insisted when he asked about its origin. Some green onion was sprinkled on the soup and a waft of ginger was enough to tell him *quelque chose de son pays* had indeed survived. When he asked her how a Vietnamese-like dish ended up here, she shrugged and said, *"Mais Monsieur, moi aussi, je suis Vietnamienne"* — But sir, I'm also Vietnamese.

But how? Impossible!

"Si, si. Depuis cinque générations, mais Vietnamienne quand même. C'était mon ancêtre qui me laissait cette recipe," she said with seriousness.

Five generations ago! Quang searched his high school memories and a piece of history made itself clear through the monotonous voice of a flint-skinned, bespectacled teacher who smoked while he lectured. *In 1888, the French exiled King Ham Nghi and his entourage when they refused to follow French rules . . .*

To who knows where.

. . . Then Prince Thanh Thai and his entourage who conspired against the French in 1907 met a similar fate . . . .

How many rebellious Vietnamese ended up here and never came back? Quang wondered. He heard the distinct whistle of his ship from a distance, but he couldn't get himself to leave. In the kitchen the refrigerator sputtered; it needed fixing. He squinted his eyes and stared at the young restaurant owner, trying to imagine her in a conical hat and a white *ao dai* dress. This mademoiselle, she grew familiar in his eyes, and Quang had to fight very hard to suppress a profound desire to reach out and caress her kinky hair.

As in all kinds of serious cooking, making pho *depends on intuition, feeling, and taste. The garnish must have it all to wake up taste buds: fresh basil and bean sprout and three kinds of chili, and wedges of lime and coriander leaves. And plum sauce for those who like it sweet.*

In Ubud, Bali, Vietnamese *pho* has taken on a delicate taste. Served with fresh snow peas and a wedge of lime and no other garnish to speak of, except a sprig of amazingly spicy basil, it's a delight to the visitor, especially when the waitress blesses the soup with a white orchid to enhance the spirit of the broth.

In Buenos Aires, an Argentine, who had been to Vietnam years ago as a doctor and knew the recipe, nursed her ailing husband who suffered from multiple sclerosis back to health solely on *pho* broth. She told the Buenos Aires *Herald* that it was a miracle cure, "but you have to cook it with absolute devotion and love and say your prayers repeatedly as the broth simmers."

In Nargakot, Nepal, high above the clouds, an Indian hotel owner whose grandfather used to live in Saigon working as a tailor, is known to serve *pho* to celebrate Vishnu every month. Though, as in India, beef is not available in Nepal and oxen meat is used as a substitute, it doesn't detract from the taste. "The meat is only a little bit more chewy, but just as good," he claims. "Plus up here, with such clear air and strong wind, everyone, the tourists, the people in town, everyone knows when my wife and I are making *pho*. Even the bloody yetis."

The lime, especially, you will pick with care, the thin-skinned ones tend to be full of juice but they rot easily. Yet nothing's more irritating than squeezing a dried-up, thick-skinned lime over a bowl of pho. *Whereas a juicy, fragrant piece of lime in its prime is heaven.*

The Vietnamese woman living in a Belgian castle was now a baroness, so Kevin learned. Once a high school teacher, she fled after the war ended. With a few gold *taels* in her pocket, she said goodbye to her mother and father and younger brother and made her way to Vung Tau and bought a seat on a crowded boat. In the dark of night, they set sail. A week or so later they ran out of food and water. A few vessels passed them by, none stopped. Some people died. Though she didn't believe in God or Buddha, the high school teacher prayed and prayed. Then a miracle: a Belgian merchant vessel took pity on their ragged S.O.S. flag and picked them up. The high school teacher was brought back to Belgium where, owning nothing, she resorted to living in the basement of a church.

She was poor, she was wretched, an exile, but she was finally free. And she was not unhappy. She did menial labor and helped clean houses and gathered wheat crops to get by. But life is strange when you cast yourself away from what you know, and who can guess what fortune will befall you from unexpected sources, especially when you are free and open to the world?

Nearby there lived a baron, a devout Catholic and a bachelor in his mid-fifties. He had wanted to be a priest but, because he was the last of his line, his family insisted he remain a layman. Still, he stayed pious and a bachelor. One day, while the baron was praying, kneeling at the front pew and staring up at the Madonna and child, the high school teacher emerged from the stairwell of the church and, well, the sunlight streaming through the stained glass window must have made her glow with a certain aura. And the baron lowered his gaze and followed her down the aisle and out of the stale church. They married. Now the mother of two children of noble blood, she would sometimes catch glimpses of herself as she glided past the gilded mirrors along the old castle's corridors and shudder, wondering, who is that? Is that me? Other times, when entertaining European royalty, she felt as if she was on a movie set and kept waiting for the director to yell: "Cut!"

When her maid brought out the steaming bowl of *pho* and as Kevin's face expressed awe and amusement, she said, "Eat, eat," and continued to tell more of her fairy-tale adventures. Wise now to love's variations and strange destinations and its endless hunger, the baroness was not unaware that another romance was about to unfold under her table: While Kevin ate, Bernard's hand was inching across that short yet impossible distance toward his ex-roommate's thigh.

When ready to serve, bring the bowls out steaming with aroma. Watch the faces of the diners: their eyes squint with anticipation, lips curve into smiles. Their delight; your reward.

On the wall of his office overlooking the Duc-Ba Cathedral in the first district, Saigon, Toan keeps a framed article he found in a fashion magazine a few years back. Among the carved jade and gold plaques that he has collected over the years, it stands alone, a treasure.

The article has a catchy riddle for a title: "Where's the Most Remote Restaurant in the World?" But it is not the answer that thrills him. No, it's the photo of a Vietnamese woman who stares past the camera with dreamy eyes to the world—the face of his true love.

Once upon a time she lived next door to him. Her bedroom he could see clearly from his balcony each morning when the curtain was pulled back, or when the wind lifted it for a second or two so as to reveal his love reading or combing her hair. Toan had recovered from the devastation of war, its horrid aftermath, had rebuilt his life after coming back from the New Economic Zone, had married, found success, but he had never recovered from a broken heart. What, after all, are ideological struggles compared to love? Perhaps it is fitting that she should come back smiling to him from a black and white photograph, after all the years.

But where was this restaurant? In a scientists' colony at the edge of Antarctica. The article told him that Nga had married, that her husband was a famous scientist, and that among glaciers and tundras and chatty penguins she grew bored. While her husband studied magnetic fields, to amuse herself, Nga made *pho*. But it had gotten so good—everyone could smell it in the colony, how could they not?—Nga ended up selling the soup as a way to buy ingredients from South America and to make more *pho*—not to make a profit, mind you, only to keep everyone around her warm and happy against the bitter cold.

Sometimes, in a whimsical mood, Toan looks at the photo and imagines himself flying over a sea of ice to see her. Just thinking about it makes his heart palpitate.

What would he say to her? Everything. A million things. Like how he ran out after her that day the communist tanks rolled into the city but he was too late: her ship had already sailed and the world as he knew it shattered. How he would have hopped on the next ship to go after her if it hadn't been for his family, his younger, helpless siblings. How he'd never had the chance to tell her how much he'd loved her. How he'd carved her initial and his on the mangosteen tree after she was gone and punched it so hard that his blood stained them forever, and how those initials have risen higher than his head. And how, despite everything, despite the changes and the years, his love for her hasn't changed.

Nga, the soup restaurant on Pasteur Street closed after your mother retired and went back to her province. A family moved in from Hanoi where you used to live and after *perestroika*, after the Cold War ended, they turned it into video parlor and it is full of kids playing those noisy electronic games. And now, last time I drove by, it's also a cyber-cafe full of smelly foreign backpackers.

The neighborhood has changed so much you wouldn't recognize it if you returned. I don't recognize it myself and I live here in Saigon. But you'll never come back, I know you. Only a handful ever return to where they used to live, and then only to look and cry a little at how the old place has fallen apart or changed, and then again they take leave.

Nga, remember those mornings when the borders were still real and even talking across the clotheslines or the courtyard was as treacherous as crossing the ocean? Yet how I long for that world! How I long for the smallness of things. Everyone knew each other then, and leaving was only for the few, not the many.

Everything has changed, Nga. Everything turned upside down. I changed. I'm a father of three, a vice president of an insurance company, the first in the country. Imagine that! I insure people against tragedy, in a country built on it.

But some things never change. I think of you. I think of you all the time. I imagine you among the howling winds. What I would give to see your face again. See how you try to guess who I could possibly be, a familiar-looking stranger standing there in front of you at the far end of the world.

But if you don't remember, if you can't recall, then I will tell you. I will remind you where we used to live, the old neighborhood, the mildewed courtyard with the mangosteen tree, and the wild parrots that fought for every fruit. Maybe you would remember. Maybe you would offer me a steaming bowl of *pho* while it is snowing outside. And I would be ravenous. I would eat like a mad man starving for decades, and you, you with your eyes always dreaming of some faraway place, would look on with amusement and approval.

And Nga, it will be the sweetest bowl of *pho* soup I'll ever taste.

Anh Dao Kolbe, "Hanoi Bamboo Wind Chimes," photograph

BRITTON GILDERSLEEVE

39A Phàn đình Phùng

I grew up in a house with bars on the windows. There were lizards on the walls, and mosquito netting moved in quiet concert with the hum of ceiling fans. I remember armed guards on my school bus. Servants who became such a part of our family that my mother wrote to them for years. A black and white dog who bit only the street boys who threw stones through the iron gates. My youngest sister spoke French before English, Vietnamese before either. Outside the second-floor sunporch the shrubs were poinsettias planted by my mother one Christmas. By the time we left they towered over the house.

When we first moved to Saigon it was still Indochina. In the interlude between French occupation and American military build-up, there were only 50 "police advisors." My father was one. But in 1960 French businessmen still rode to work in cyclos, there were as many four-star restaurants as French lycées, and almost no one foresaw body bags.

War came, but I remember frangipani. Climbing high into the twisted branches, battling the ants for sweetly heady blossoms. My favorite tree bloomed in the yard down the street. It belonged— does love entitle one to ownership?—to Dr. McIntyre. My mother would go to visit, calling cards in white-gloved hands, and while she sipped cool drinks I would climb into the frangipani. The ants would trace their purposeful paths along the shiny bark while I watched. They moved in quiet single file, precisely measured like the increments on a ruler. If you put a leaf over their path, the ants coalesced into small patrols, and the leader ants would pass back information through coded movements of their tiny antennae.

There were Sunday drives with the chauffeur—our cook's husband—on the infamous Bien Hoa highway. The highway unfurled before our blue and white Buick like ribbon on a promised present. Vietnam was twenty-two shades of green, I once heard a Marine say. There were emerald hills that folded on themselves like a cloak draped negligently over a voluptuous woman. Rice paddies the color of alfalfa clover flanked either side of the highway: farmers herded water buffalo along the ridges separating window-pane fields. Yoked teams occasionally stopped our passing. We would hang out the windows and wave as the barefoot man, woman or child shooed the beasts down the slope into the muddy green water below.

Entire families were transported on bicycles. A father pedalling his wife, their toddler and infant cocooned between them. An old woman in her black *ao ∂ai*, its split skirts neatly tucked under her hips as she rode side-saddle behind her suit-clad grandson. Petal-faced young women, their glossy black hair like banners of quiet defiance in the tropical breeze. Motorcycles could carry an almost inconceivable number of people: at least five, more if it were a Lambretta with a step-through frame. Buses were equally heavy-laden. Old women, their teeth stained blood-black from betel nut, would hang out the rusty doorways. From every window. . . a basket, a package, a wide-brimmed straw hat. Yet Vietnam never felt crowded to me. Middle Eastern cities—even other former French colonies like Algiers—can be so oppressive that a friend of mine coined the phrase "man-swarm" for the surging hordes. If Algiers was an oil painting, Saigon was a watercolor.

We had two amahs. One for the baby: "old" ChiBa. She was probably in her 20s. My sister Diane was ChiBa's private preserve. I lost one bedroom to the nursery's preparation. The next fell to ChiBa; she insisted on being close to *la petite*. I ended up in a cubby we formerly used to house the wardrobes. ChiBa would terrify us with Vietnamese ghost stories. If you left your bed in the middle of the night—never mind the reason—there was a demon underneath your bed. It would bite your ankles horribly. My second sister wet the bed until she was almost nine. It was impossible to brave ChiBa's chillingly convincing devil.

Our second amah—ChiBon—took care of us three older girls. Afternoons or vacation days she would walk us around the corner to the Vietnamese American Association library, where her friends from university studied and practiced English. At the VAA the slender girls in their graceful *ao ∂ais* would giggle at us, gently teasing my sister Dori about being Doris Day. It was a standing joke they never tired of.

ChiBon took us to her family's farm. Children ran after chickens; water buffalo swayed in a large paddock. Intricate hand-woven baskets held produce, ducks. It was a paradise for city kids, who were able to ride their bicycles only on the grounds outside the President's palace. We abandoned our shoes and ran into the mud that was the very floor of Vietnam, the silty, velvety mud that underlay rice paddies and paddocks and war.

It was a safe time. There were tanks clattering past the house's iron gate, and soldiers, and bombings at the movie theatre. But I remember getting up early in the pre-dawn stillness, slipping down the stairs, and running in my nightgown through the city's empty streets with my dog. It was still dark. You could smell the street waking up, damp and cool before the onslaught of tropical heat. I thought I was flying, racing the dawn behind a black and white dog. I was 10 years old.

The city streets were beautiful, lined with trees I've never found elsewhere. They bore a miserable fruit which dropped into a curdled mess on the driveway. I was allergic to it and broke out in a rash. But the trees formed almost a tunnel over the pavement, shading the street before the drive as if it were a boulevard in Paris.

Flowers grew everywhere. They lined Flower Street, stalls of glorious exuberant color, strong and clear. The intoxicating plumeria, orchids, banana trees, flame trees in yellow and red, and a fragile translucent white flower I pressed between the pages of my Bible. Its perfect petals lie behind my father's scrawled inscription. Lizards bloomed on the walls like more exotic flora. The prettiest ones—blue-headed, yellow-bellied and all the rainbow in between—were poisonous, someone told me once.

Sometimes on Sunday my father would take us to the *Cercle Sportif*, the sports club, to play in the sandbox. My father traveled—Câp St. Jacques, which later became Vung Tau; Da Nang; Dalat. He was seldom home. His Sunday afternoons not traveling were the time Daddy spent with us. He would drive us to the club in the blue and white Buick, and watch us swing. The three older fair-skinned daughters in pastel dresses, big skirts rising on the swings like fragile bubbles on the fretful breeze.

Some days one of the servants—usually ChiBon—would take us to the zoo. The infamous tiger cages: I remember only the tigers, how strong and feral they were, pacing back and forth. And the yellow-bibbed bears on Bear Island, waving to us from across their moat. If we had money we would buy sugar cane to feed the elephants, watching their deft trunks loop around the stalks held breathlessly in our outstretched hands, then slowly crunched, inch by inch, into their triangular mouths.

There was a Buddhist temple carved from a living banyan tree. Inside you could give the monk a *piastre* and he would light a joss stick. Heavy incense would fill the already smoky interior and filter through the temple's walls, ropy from the twisted banyan trunks. It seemed an appropriate residence, somehow, for a god that delighted in the tiny paper clothes burned each New Year for the dead. When I returned to the U.S., I wondered how God could live within the white confines of church.

There were ox carts, lumbering wagons pulled by ponderous Brahmans. Humps towered over swaying wattles, and the animals would watch you from their wise sloe eyes. Monks came at dawn, their golden robes rhyming with the honey sunlight. Even the Catholic cook bowed her obeisance, proffering a bowl of some savory mixture of rice and vegetables. Fruit vendors, vegetable men, women with baskets of sweet dumplings: their distinctive cries wove through the house like the refrain to a familiar melody. Counterpoint harmony was someone—the noodle man?—clacking two sticks together in his own individual rhythm.

The market was always *le grand marché*. In the traditional fashion, certain alleys sold specific items: the lacquer alleys, the material market, rattan and baskets. Vegetables were in one area, fruit in another. Fish would announce their alley long before you reached it mid-morning. Strolling vendors vied with lepers for attention, and starving mothers pushed forward big-bellied chil- dren, who stretched out hands to stroke blond hair. Appeal was everywhere, mute or vocal.

There remain pictures. My mother gave me one of the lacquer photo albums the Vietnamese artisans crafted so carefully. The lacquer process was similar to the Chinese style—countless painstaking coats, applied meticulously for a depth of color impos- sible to attain now; a Vietnamese friend told me that art is lost. A gold and tortoise fish on the album's glossy black front cover swims through a stylized tangle of fronds to its mate.

I remember going to the market with my mother to buy that album. There were two: one large, one small. She kept the larger one and gave me the smaller one as a gift many years later. I opened the box and sat, silent. My mother asked me if I minded that the album had been hers. So many of my memories of Vietnam are my mother's: the white-glove teas at the ambassador's resi- dence; copper-plate calling-cards marking the rite of passage into adolescence; bridge parties, cocktail parties, dinner parties; women in swirling dresses, men in evening clothes. The patina of expectations duly met.

I didn't have photos of Vietnam when my mother gave me the album. I saved it for many years, waiting for the polishing of memories, the surfacing of perfect photos. Years later, when I too was an expatriate, I found us: the baby, the toddler, and two blond girls standing smiling before the screened verandah. A sulky Doris Day and her leggy older sister curled in rattan furniture as ChiBa and ChiBon watched over us.

By then the album was in storage. I placed my childhood within other pages. But when I turn those pages, I see my tortoise fish, swimming gracefully to his mate. A thousand miles away, he still swims.

I don't remember leaving. I remember only being gone. Returning to a world where we didn't belong: funny clothes, funny accents, and the sense of global citizenship too natural to expatriate children. Years later, when newspapers carried the news that Saigon was to be re-named Ho Chi Minh City, I realized why the memory of leaving is so vague—I never left. Some part of me remains, a young girl running in the streets of pre-war Saigon. Like the city with the new name, that child lives unchanged within the woman who raises expatriate children of her own. She waves to me, a nightgowned ghost safe behind a black and white dog, still running through the streets.

Anh Dao Kolbe, "Hue-Dien Tho Pink," photograph

PATRICK COLE

The Draft

We didn't know it—we didn't know anything—but the school was growing. Over the preceding few years, class sizes had burgeoned, topping thirty pupils in each. They had to use the gymnasium as an extra cafeteria in the middle of the day and long-vacant rooms in the basement were used as classrooms. We didn't know it, but our school was built in the fifties and these basement rooms were intended as bomb shelters. Our third-grade social studies class was in one of the shelters, the one right next to the boiler room.

The boiler—we never saw it, but it was giant, we knew it as an ominous thing. Its name alone suggested it, ballooning power, stretching stitches, barely contained explosions, one after another, all day long, all during the school year. We knew it heated the building, an awesome task. During the summer, we presumed, it rested. The boiler was something beyond our reach, our understanding, something for adults, one of their just-controlled monsters, Frankenstein. We imagined the boiler black and greasy and full of fire shadows, a locomotive engine. Some sweating, skinny old janitor with stained overalls covered in black soot might shovel in its fuel—an act of homage, of propitiation.

We didn't know the boiler was quite old, outdated, that it had warmed thousands of unseen children as they filed past year after year. We did not know that the school district did not have the money to replace it, that they were waiting for it to die, so raw need would justify the expense.

We never saw it. What we knew about it we learned from what we heard from it in our social studies class. It was just on the other side of the blackboard we all faced, lined up as we were in rows. The blackboard covered most of the wall in front of us. It was washed clean every evening, and in the morning when we went to our first class, social studies, it faced us like a blank screen. It was a liquid dark, like a hole, a hole you could reach through or get sucked into, an infinite abyss, a hole punched into the wall, into the school, into our lives, into life. And from the other side came the grand clanks and heavy exhalations, low roaring and grumphing punctuated now and then by a sudden metal shriek.

We didn't know our school was crowded. We didn't know having class in the basement and eating in the gym was a desperate thing, an unplanned thing, a jury-rigged thing. Because we were in the third grade. To us, the planet was as it was because it had been arranged that way. Everything according to a plan now near completion. Completed. Or, everything that was left was just mopping up. Things were as they were because that was how they were; presumably sometime in the past it had been decided that this would be the best result. Things weren't worsening or getting better or even changing at all, they were just *being*. What kind of world would it be if things were always changing, if there wasn't a solid jungle-gym of solid being for us, in which we could play, act out our lives, as we wanted, unmolested by vacillating circumstances? Circumstances were to be the monkey bars, hollow structures made of firm metal pieces which never moved, which supported us in our climbing and sitting and in whatever wild gyrations we were inspired to do.

We didn't imagine the world could, or should, be changed. We were fortunate to have been born so near the end of time.

Here's something we did know but which held absolutely no significance: it was 1976. 1976—hieroglyphics! It could have been any number—312, 872, 1648. 3236. 111. Same thing. 0.

Our social studies teacher was Mr. Stuhby, pronounced "Stooby." He had his work cut out for him—his task was to introduce us to other countries, faraway lands, and somehow convince us that they existed. That there were people there who ate different things. Spoke different languages. *Looked* different. Countries that didn't have space programs. Countries that didn't make all of their own food, that had trouble—believe it or not—feeding their children. Countries with weird shapes, weird names.

One thing that made it more likely that other nations existed, anyway, was that all of the world's countries seemed to be up to the same thing. All were on board with the rest, at least, in that they had imports and exports. Wheat, oranges, bauxite—whatever that was—cereals (like breakfast cereals?), grains, minerals. Ore. As proof, we were shown pictures of all these places and maps with little symbols for wheat and bauxite here and there, near the mountains or the plains. This was the world—a bunch of countries stuck together, countries at work, farming, mining, building industries, importing, exporting. Feeding. Starving. A lot of activity.

We didn't buy any of it.

Give us a break—there was danger in coming to believe that these countries existed, here at the end of time. That they were different from our country. They introduced imperfection into the system. If they were different, there was imperfection in the world—our country was perfect, how could there be more than one type of perfection? And if they had overt problems, wicked storms, droughts, lack—then there was imperfection in the world. Something was wrong with the end of time.

The opposite explanation presents itself quite naturally, too. This is, of course, that the world *was* perfect, it was the end of time. Our country was perfect. And if other nations starved or warred, lived poorly or died needlessly, that was all part of the great plan, too. How it was supposed to be. That was a perfect world, too.

Mr. Stuhby was an interesting character. He had straight black hair which came down from the sides of his head to cover his ears and thick sideburns of tangled black hair, dense blackbird nests. He wore thick-rimmed, brown rectangular glasses. His wisdom, we figured intuitively, probably derived from his great age. And Mr. Stuhby was always smiling, smiling as if it was funny, and fun, to be a third-grade teacher. Or to be a third-grade student. Or to be anybody.

Mr. Stuhby was famous, as it were. That is, he was popular, and we had all heard about him from older siblings and students. When we said we were now in Mr. Stuhby's class, it was as if we had arrived, and all of our older brothers and sisters and the older students would not stop smiling.

Don't misunderstand: Mr. Stuhby was not the great teacher one hears about. The one people refer back to, talking about how he or she helped them out. Steered them clear of problems, steered them into the profession they loved. No. It's just that now we see that he was responsible for a few important things.

Mr. Stuhby, believe it or not, had actually been to some of these weird countries we talked about in class. The older students, especially, knew that he had been to one of these countries in particular.

Our lives were peaceful. There was nothing left to be done, in our neighborhoods, in our state, in our country, in the world. Work wasn't necessary, school wasn't even necessary, no one ever gave us a reason for it, we only went to please the adults. To give them some time to themselves, to do whatever it was they were doing— shoring up some last loose ends to the smoothing of the world, probably. So we wouldn't have to. Best to let them do it.

Our lives were peaceful. Of course, we had all fallen in love once, mostly in the second grade, but even that did not challenge our view of the world. We would see another one of us day after day at school, and then suddenly they would start to glow. They would start to seem different from the rest of us, perfect. This fact was encoded in their name, it was the name of this thing, *Heather*, *Josh*, *Billy*, *Jennifer*, and we understood it. They had to have just the name they had because it indicated not who they were but what they were. The one we loved.

They would make us feel soft, quieted, but excited. We would want more. More of what, we couldn't say. We knew the word for this indescribable thing, we knew it was love.

Spaces were opened up inside, spaces like hot, humid caves. We would start to daydream. We would ride the school bus home very sadly, going to our nightly separation from the "one." At home, songs repeated on the radio would remind us of the one we loved in our class. This verified our experience as love—we knew that adults had such feelings triggered by music—hell, sometimes the songs triggering the feelings would talk about songs triggering the feeling. So we would imagine running away with the "one." The only place we knew away from home was school, so we would imagine running away there, living there in secret, in the secret places on the playground which we thought no one knew of. We would live there with our chosen one and be left alone by every- one, adults, other children, the world.

The fantasy persisted for a while, but we knew deep down it made no sense. How long could we live at the playground? How would we get food? How would we stay warm? Would it be enough to just be together, forever?

We only knew what we felt. It couldn't be doubted. We marveled at the fact that the feeling actually did seem localized in the heart—we knew exactly where that was because of the Pledge of Allegiance, when we put our right hands on our hearts every morning at school. The heart was not a metaphor at all. It was a real thing. Just like the popular songs said. Feeling liquid adrenaline pain there meant you weren't making the whole thing up, it wasn't all in your head, you were really in something, perceiving something bigger than you, outside your head, true love, real love. The heart was the independent observer. The litmus test, the bullshit detector.

But our daydreams quickly came to dead-ends. The feeling was one thing, but doing something, reacting to the feeling, was another matter. There were a lot of distractions, too—everything around us reminded us of the real world, where we belonged, with the other children. The other children, finger-painting, sliding down slides, getting sick on the merry-go-round, getting pushed down by a bully, raising hands, having to go to the bathroom, *running* to the cafeteria, collecting stickers, being tempted to steal a neighbor's eraser. The other children, none of them distracted from wholeheartedly being children, kids. Time went on, and we waited to see what would happen next. Something would take care of it, as our parents took care of everything invisibly. The feeling had come from nowhere, the next step in dealing with it would too. So we waited. What was weird about love was that it pushed us to the future, it made us imagine a future circumstance, or to anticipate a future circumstance. Clearly, with love, something was coming. Feeling it was a beginning. We waited, feeling love, feeling love, feeling it, until…a funny thing happened. It went away like the hiccups.

But still our lives were peaceful. We knew it was 1976 and it was the bicentennial year, whatever that meant—it was something good, we were assured, some kind of proof of something—and we were children and that was perfect and in our first period class we had recently heard of, or learned about, a country rather suspiciously named Turkey which had a great deal of cotton and wool to sell. That hadn't really sunk in, the Turkey thing. It was more like a rumor. So everything was fine and normal, as always.

It is no wonder that irregularity frightened us. A big part of perfection is that it is predictable. Mr. Stuhby coming in late for class in the morning was hard to incorporate into our idea of the world, which was really no idea, no idea was necessary, an idea of the world wasn't necessary if the world was perfect. Mr. Stuhby coming in late for class in the morning would be the introduction of an idea into a sea of no ideas, a void. And it happened. We had an unknown teacher, an alien, sitting to one side, watching us. We had already said the Pledge of Allegiance, crossed our hearts and hoped to die. And then we waited. It was odd, given that we assumed Mr. Stuhby lived somewhere in the building with all the other teachers. But minutes passed and we sat in silence and could hear the clock over the door buzzing continuously and he was still not there. The never-ending blackboard shined in front of us. We stared at it. Unblocked by the presence of a teacher, an adult protector, it yawned wide. Behind it the boiler clanged. It groaned, clanged again.

Mr. Stuhby entered at last, a full fifteen minutes late — an eternity. He did not looked disturbed, or as if whatever had detained him had indeed been something wrong, an accident, something out of line with the plan. In fact, he seemed to be smiling more widely than usual as he went to the big wooden desk which faced us from the front of the classroom, dismissed the watcher, arranged some papers, selected one, then walked to the front. Finally he stood in front of the middle of the blackboard, blocking it, paused a moment to look around at us, and then said an incredible thing.

"Vietnam!"

There it is. Vietnam.

We were now going to learn the meaning of this word. It would then have a special power for us. Now when we heard it, instead of skating along on a simple, literal, two-dimensional definition of it, we would automatically feel a deeper, truer meaning. We can't help it. We are children with this word, when this word is in the air. We are children again, in touch.

You know how they say children are like sponges. They just soak everything up. We soaked up Vietnam. Without even knowing we were doing it.

Vietnam is like a magic password, abracadabra hocus-pocus *Vietnam!* Saying it or even just thinking it brings something into the world. It is immediate, it is all there at once, it does not require thought, understanding. It is the music of Chopin, it is about what it is. What it means can be explained only to those who already understand it.

When we see the word Vietnam, the letters smile at us, that big capital V like a grin, a sharpened tooth, Churchill's chubby Victory, a confident, fat smile wrapped all around in black. The word looks weird, it looks fun, there is some kind of provocative invitation, an indulgence, a thrill, macabre excitement. Vietnam — some kind of wildness, drama, importance.

It is one of those illicit words hidden — hiding — in one of the sections at the back of the dictionary for little-used, exotic letters; the shunned, the castigated, the strange, unplaceable, uncategorizable, unknown creatures which exist and to which some of us are drawn, as if we know them, and they us.

So odd, but eminently pronounceable, easier than American words –

V

et

nam

!

Vietnam — it attracts. It draws you in. You can never let go. Like coming across a shining jewel in a patch of mud:

Mrrrrnnneoblleckrrghhhhahhmmmmmphvietnamgrrrawwwwehhhooo-onooomotherr . . .

Vietnam! He asked us what we knew about it. No one raised a hand. We knew nothing about it. We were in the third grade; we had never encountered it. By chance, but not surprisingly, no one in the class had a mommy or daddy who had been there. So we were quiet. The boiler exhaled uneasily behind Mr. Stuhby.

"Nothing," he said, smiling. "Well, don't feel bad." We didn't. "Until quite recently, no one in this country knew anything about Vietnam.

"But now it's different. Now it's important to know about Vietnam. Now everyone knows more than they'd like to about Vietnam." He went to the side of the classroom, where there was a map of the world. The liquid blackboard opened out in front of us again, unobstructed.

The map was on a stand like that used for a portable film screen. Mr. Stuhby turned it towards us, asked who could identify the United States on it.

Some of us raised our hands. Some of us knew the answer very well, and were very eager to give it. Some of us waited patiently to be called upon, others pointed and shouted, "There it is!"

There it was. The United States. U.S.A. Hey, presto!

That shape—a meaning. A meaning in itself. It seemed to face east, with all of New England an arm extending up over the rest of it like the arm of the goddamn Statue of Liberty itself. A thick, strong arm, a neck, with a wise face on Maine with noble features there out in front of the rest of the country, the eagle's beak, the pulpit of a ship heading out into the Atlantic, inspecting the waters ahead first, looking back sternly but approvingly over its shoulder at the rest of the country, calming it, steadying it, protecting.

That shape—so random, made of arbitrary straight lines, forgotten treaties, broken treaties, eroding ocean coastlines, permanently meandering rivers—it made sense. It was where and how it should be. It was, of course, perfect. We were proud, in a nascent way, with a pride that felt like the love we had in the second grade.

"Now where is Vietnam?"

He waited a few moments and then pointed it out. It surprised us, how quickly he pointed to it. He had no trouble finding it, even though it was small, unknown, nonexistent. He pointed to it right away—it was right where it should be, apparently. Right where he left it. Right where it left him. The shape of Vietnam—a ragged, upside-down question mark. It made no sense to us. It too was like the love we felt in the second grade. A reality with which we didn't know yet what to do.

A banging came from the blackboard. We looked to it, it muttered something to itself.

"Vietnam used to be two countries, like it shows here on the map. It was easy to remember: one was called *North* Vietnam and the other was called *South* Vietnam. But this is no longer so. To make it even easier for us Americans, they got the two together, so now there's just one *Vietnam*. And you all are very lucky, because I can tell you quite a bit about Vietnam from first-hand experience, because I have been there, when I was a soldier in the United States Army."

We were astonished. It was astonishing that a teacher had ever been anywhere outside the school. It was astonishing that a teacher had ever been anything other than a teacher. And being a soldier—it was romantic. It was like being a kid, even though you were grown up—you were kept apart from the usual humdrum adult world. It was like childhood. The emphasis seemed to be on being outside a lot, and on excitement. There was running around. There was mud. There were jungle gyms. There were sports, like shooting. You were indulged. You got a uniform, but it didn't serve to show how you were just like so many others, it showed how you were different from those without a uniform. You were special. It was like your special day, every day. There was no messiness associated with the job, no pain or blood or humiliation—somehow, in our minds, it was all part of the perfect world, too.

It was also astonishing that a teacher would mention such an experience, such a past life. This was not what teachers did. This was not what adults did. It didn't scare us; it just astounded us. Mr. Stuhby was changing right before our eyes. He was adding dimensions. Mr. Stuhby was becoming *Mr. Stuhby*, the one we would know from then on. This was the Mr. Stuhby that made people smile when they thought of him. The old one, poor Mr. Stuhby, would disappear forever.

Still, this all had to be part of the perfect plan. We were confident it would turn out to be so. Then we'd have a laugh.

"But let's start from the start. Normally, we'd just open our textbooks and turn to the chapter on Vietnam. But our textbooks are old and outdated." Outdated? "Things have changed since the book was written. So I've prepared a little introduction on the country which I am going to read to you. Pay close attention."

The disgruntled blackboard beside Mr. Stuhby hissed. Taken aback by the unusual introduction to this fictional country, we gave him our full attention. When he saw that this was so, Mr. Stuhby began. Like conducting an orchestra. Standing alongside the map, he smiled as he spoke and he spoke very slowly, very deliberately.

"Vietnam." *Abracadabra.* "Vietnam, Vietnam, Vietnam." He paused, glancing up at us. Our minds started going blank. It was such an odd sound, *Vietnam*. It didn't seem real, but he insisted. "Vietnam is a very beautiful country in Southeast Asia." Our eyes, glued to Mr. Stuhby's smiling face, began to glaze.

"Vietnam is bordered by China, Cambodia, and Laos. The population of Vietnam is sixty million." Sixty million seemed like a lot. A huge number. A heavy number, a tiring number. It weighed us down, *sixty million*. We couldn't help it, we felt drained, dazed. We were vaguely aware of the blackboard, it was mumbling behind Mr. Stuhby, while he carried on, smiling: "The capital of

Vietnam is now Hanoi. Hanoi is a large city of nearly one million inhabitants." Another heavy million. Millions, millions, millions . . . .

The depthless blackboard suddenly clanged loudly. We looked to it with anguished faces as the clanging rang, our ears rang, and the noise drowned everything out, including Mr. Stuhby's voice. When the ringing subsided, we heard more groaning from the blackhole blackboard. We were only vaguely aware of Mr. Stuhby, as now it seemed it was he who was mumbling, saying again something about millions. Now more than ever the blackboard seemed to be in control, the focus of the room, the reason for it, the heart of the school, the purpose, as if the classroom and afterwards the entire school building were built around it, it was there first, it had always been there, an ancient thing polished to shiny black by centuries. We felt the pull of the blackboard. The groaning subsided and a ticking sound came from it. Things were happening in there. The ticking grew louder, faster. And now Mr. Stuhby was there. He was stepping off a large airplane into a fierce rain. Before long he was soaked and stepping though thick mud a foot deep. Someone beside him said, They never said anything about *rain*.

"The land in Vietnam is made up mostly of hills and mountains with thick forests and jungle covering them, though the coastal plain is flat. Rice is cultivated in the mountain valleys. The main exports of the country are rice, rubber, coal, wood, fish, tea, and coffee. Vietnam imports oil, fertilizers, and steel."

The blackboard retched. Mr. Stuhby was walking down a dirt road. It was getting dark, and several others were walking with him, though they were several feet from each other. They had been walking for hours. It was deeply monotonous. Mr. Stuhby looked to his left and right, noticing, as he had several times before, that some of the men were not walking in the road but alongside it. He lightly wondered why, given that it must be easier to walk in the road than along the overgrown sides. One droning minute passed: there was an explosion. Someone walking five feet directly behind him had tripped a mine. Mr. Stuhby felt small pieces of metal slice his wrist and strafe the back of his legs. He turned and saw a soldier face-up on the ground, bloody, his right leg separated from his body. There were shouts for the medic, who came running from the front of the group. The medic stripped off all unnecessary items as he ran, his pack, his helmet, his poncho, and when he got to the wounded man his chest and head were bare and he carried only his medical bag. He then went calmly about his business.

48

"Major industries in Vietnam include coal, cement, paper, and cloth. In addition, Vietnam makes use of its long coastline to produce great quantities of fish sauce and other processed seafood products."

There was a *pinging* sound. It was flying past Mr. Stuhby's ears, over and over again. It was a clear, sunny day, and Mr. Stuhby and his patrol had been spotted by the enemy, before they had spotted them. He stood still wondering over the pinging sound, until the platoon leader tackled him. He honestly did not know what bullets in flight sounded like until that moment.

After crawling off the trail to cover in thick, high grass, he and his platoon came to realize they were heavily outnumbered. They stayed down, as low as possible, and waited for the enemy to approach.

Mr. Stuhby lay flat on his belly and waited. He was scared, but in control. He heard Viet Cong approaching cautiously. One passed within six feet of him, but Mr. Stuhby did not fire, he made no sound, no movements. He then became aware of a strange, repulsive sensation on his left leg. Soon he felt it on his right leg, then his thighs, his waist, his chest, his neck. He was acrawl in fire ants. They stung him all over. Still he made no sounds or movements. Several moments passed. Eventually they added up to five minutes. The Viet Cong moved on, disappearing into the vegetation as rapidly as they had appeared.

Ever since, including the day he stood before his third-grade class, saying "Vietnam has many religions," our ever-smiling Mr. Stuhby was not ticklish on any part of his body.

"Vietnam has many religions. Buddhism, a religion common in Asia, is one. There are several other religious groups there, including a large community of Christians."

Hue. *Way.* The Way. The Way City. No Way City. Way-Out City. The Way of Life City, The Way of Death City. Have Thine Own Hue. Hue City.

Mr. Stuhby was crouched behind a bullet-pocked wall, inching his way along towards a bridge spanning a dirty brown river, thinking about words. You could say them in one language, and they floated up in the air, and then someone else could retrieve them in another language. They did it all the time. After seven months, Vietnamese words peppered his speech, like Army acronyms did—*đi đi, titi, đinky đow*. And now, *Tet*. Tet Tet-Tet Tet. It sounded like automatic weapons fire.

He thought about it some more, Tet Tet-Tet Tet. Then he realized that this time it *was* automatic weapons fire. Here we go again, here we go, he said to himself. A few more pockmarks showed up on the wall beside him. Why? Mr. Stuhby thought, crouching down further. Why me? Why am I here? In this insane place? Why not someone else? Why me? Will I ever really get back to the World? I've been here seven months, got 152 days left. 1-5-2. Forever. Been here forever, gonna be here forever. I still don't get it. I just don't get it. Why? Why me?

Mr. Stuhby made his way forward towards the river. Bent over, he came to the body of a young Vietnamese woman. At first he recognized her only as an object to crouch near for a pause, to scan the area a moment before moving on. After stopping he saw that the body was a body and looked at her for a second. "Numbah ten," he heard in his head, in a female Vietnamese accent, like he had heard many times before. They catch our words, too, he thought. He regarded the woman's face. At her age, it would be surprising if she didn't have children. Why her? He thought. Why me? Why her? *Why*—it had started to sound to him like a Vietnamese word. The firing was growing louder, more rapid up ahead. He looked around and then back down at the woman's face. "Hue," he said to her, before jogging forward a few more steps.

"The weather is generally hot and humid, as Vietnam has a tropical climate. Every year, the country receives vast amounts of rain during the rainy, or monsoon, season."

The blackboard moaned a great bellyache. It *hueyed*, then it *teted*. Mr. Stuhby watched as a gunboat moving rapidly down the river before him suddenly exploded. All of it, at once. It was an amazing sight, and Mr. Stuhby instinctively thought he was glad, he was lucky, to have seen it.

Seconds later, our third-grade teacher was running onto the metal bridge crossing the river. There was heavy fire on the other side. It was chaos. He saw some Marines up ahead trying to make their way back onto the bridge. He saw some Marines lying still around him. One of the Marines up ahead came running onto the bridge. He was shouting at Mr. Stuhby but Mr. Stuhby could not hear him for the gunfire and its echoing off the metal bridge. The Marine got to Mr. Stuhby and yanked him forward. He steered Mr. Stuhby through raining fire down the opposite end of the bridge, past retreating Marines, before pulling him down beside a man lying on a stretcher. The man was a Navy corpsman, a medic assigned to a Marine platoon. He had been shot in the back, and was paralyzed from the waist down. He was still conscious; there were many more wounded to be attended to, and no one else could do it. The Marine wanted Mr. Stuhby to pick up the other end of the stretcher on which the corpsman lay, so they both could ferry the corpsman around to the wounded, so the corpsman could lean over and patch them up. After the Marine explained the situation, the corpsman looked up at Mr. Stuhby and shouted, "Let's go!"

They ran him from downed Marine to downed Marine. The corpsman went about his work as if nothing had happened to him. Mr. Stuhby and the Marine carrying the other end of the stretcher tried to help as much as they could with the corpsman's work, ripping off clothes, applying compresses, following whatever instructions the corpsman shouted. When they set the stretcher down next to the fifth wounded Marine they had been to, the corpsman shouted for Mr. Stuhby to get behind him and prop him up. Mr. Stuhby ran behind the corpsman, lifted him up by the shoulders, and leaned against his body so he that was sitting up somewhat. The corpsman started treating a bullet wound in the downed man's abdomen. Mr. Stuhby examined the wounded man's face. He was very pale, and seemed confused. Then the wounded man looked up at the corpsman. He recognized him.

"Dave," he said, "am I dead?"

The corpsman started laughing while he worked. He said, "If you are, Marty, then so am I," and at that moment the corpsman took a shot in the chest, another in the leg, and first went tense, and tense for another moment, then limp, in Mr. Stuhby's arms.

The blackboard sighed, and then there was quiet.

The clock over the door buzzed. Eventually we noticed it. We had no idea how long it had been silent in the room except for that clock buzzing. It seemed like days, weeks had passed. We steered our heads away from the blackboard and refocused our eyes on our teacher, Mr. Stuhby. He was sitting at the big wooden desk. His mouth was closed, but he was smiling.

"There it is," Mr. Stuhby said. "That's basically Vietnam. So let's take a break."

Vietnam—see it? What is shining behind it, through it? We know what, but we can't tell you what it is.

Transfixed by the light from behind it, we cannot place its literal meaning. Cannot remember its shape (the upside-down question mark), cannot recall its placement on a map (right where it should be), cannot tell you about its imports and exports (people). The instant you ask what it means, you have lost the ability to understand it. So don't think. Listen.

Just the beginning—*Vi*—like a screech, a dentist's shrill drill, it makes our teeth float.

See how there in the forest of that word, in the treeline of Vietnam, things are moving, all kinds of things, out-of-place things, horizontal lines, all kinds of things are running around in there, in between the letters, in between the sounds, in *Vi—et—nam.*

It is like a word with a meaning we once forgot, but which we all once knew, and now we have remembered again. The quintessential word, Vietnam. The archetypal word, Vietnam. The first word there was, so regular, the syllables, it spills out and along so easily, like a snake from a tree, of its own clear and obvious momentum—it must mean something. This construction itself implies great meaning, this natural tumbling of simple sounds, it suggests meaning, great meaning, in itself, as the sky is itself transcendent, suggesting something other, something beyond: an eye, a god.

As if it were, Vietnam, the most ancient of words, buried in dry yellow sandstone tombs for centuries and recently uncovered. Having never seen it, we recognize it still.

It is amazing that it can be written by anyone, even a child, that just anyone can cobble together the forms which make such a thing. It is amazing it can be written at all.

Or misspell it: Vtnam, Vietnm, Vitnam—it's still there, defying its injury to shout itself.

We try to give it a new meaning, new meanings. But the old, unspeakable thing shines through it always.

"It's a beautiful day today, isn't it?" Mr. Stuhby said, gesturing towards the windowless wall. We looked there, and he described the scene for us while the blackboard's stomach gurgled. There was the playground, empty of children, each swing empty, available, all hanging perfectly still. The ground around the swings, the monkey bars, the merry-go-round, were all patches of yellow dust. Under the swings there were deep grooves in the dirt, carved by our braking feet.

It was indeed a beautiful day, sunny, blue, clouds here and there placed with the precise accidental regularity of an impressionist painter. The empty playground seemed to call out for us, for our laughing and running and picking on each other and hanging upside down and showing off.

"Well then," Mr. Stuhby said, turning our eyes and cleared minds back into the classroom. "We've had our little introduction to Vietnam." At the mention of the word, we were jolted. We felt it, *Vietnam*. But though the feeling was strong, it was not yet permanent. Something was missing—our hearts hadn't yet verified it.

Mr. Stuhby knew we believed him, we believed everything he said, all the time. We had no reason to doubt teachers or adults in general. We believed Mr. Stuhby when he told us he had been to Vietnam. And yet, it wasn't quite true. Mr. Stuhby was still just a teacher who lived in the school building, he had never been outside of it, he had never been a soldier, and Vietnam wasn't real either, it was just the name of another make-believe country the adults told us about to give us something to do. We were still in the third grade, submerged in 1976. The world was perfect and done and organized and of course there was a limit to the number and variety of things in it—only those things right in front of you existed and were part of the plan. Hell, some of us were from broken homes, but we still believed it. Such prejudice is hard to overcome.

Even though we felt something new, something unsettling, there was still some disconnect: we believed Mr. Stuhby, but in a one-dimensional way, a way which never would have stood up to someone asking, Do you *really* believe what Mr. Stuhby has said? That would have led to a roadblock: Well, yes, but, no…? A contradiction we wouldn't have been able to handle. The way of our belief was unaccustomed to scrutiny. Didn't utilize it, and never expected it to come from outside, either. What use has scrutiny in a perfect world? Children that we were, we were comfortable *saying* that we believed in Mr. Stuhby, and in what we now felt, without really believing in it. There was no contradiction for us.

So there was a gap between our belief and reality—they were still separate things and not united. You could trace the pathway of belief to reality and find that the fault lay in our imagination. There was a canyon there, between belief and reality, that needed a bridge. Mr. Stuhby now offered to fix that short-circuit.

We had no idea what the long-term effects of this bridging would be. That many, many other things would cross. That there was no undoing it.

"Now who would like to learn more about Vietnam?" he asked. We all raised our hands. We knew it was the right answer.

Mr. Stuhby looked around the room. He paused for a moment. He was making a diagnosis. He was judging the winds. He was looking over the crops from the porch at the close of day. "I tell you what then," he said. "Tomorrow I'll bring in my draft card. My draft card was sent to me by the government. It was my order to go to Vietnam. My ticket, you might say. I'll bring it in tomorrow. How would you like that?"

We couldn't believe it. This strange card purported to show that Mr. Stuhby actually was in the Army, that he actually had been a soldier. That he had actually been to Vietnam—and therefore, Vietnam existed. But there was more—here, in school, we were going to see something real. Some actual *proof*. Proof that all the things thrown at us were out there somewhere beyond the confines of the building or the covers of the textbook, with its stylized symbols for minerals and grains.

We all said we would very much like to see this card. This official document from the *government* proving the existence of Vietnam, of all we had learned Vietnam to be. It was a threat to the perfect edifice of the world, sure. But we didn't think of that. Emotional and rash as we were, we trusted our curiosity. And we had no idea of the true significance of this moment, of coming to believe in Vietnam. For one thing, we did not know that Vietnam would never be mentioned again in school, for the remaining nine years. Mentioning Vietnam then would be like mentioning Bigfoot or the Loch Ness Monster, as if it was a lie, a fantasy, as if there was no proof. Because every year we would start history from the start again, in the fall, with the colonial days, pass quickly to the heroism of the Revolution, onwards through the nineteenth century, and generally finish, in the spring, with the heroism of World War Two. At that point, year after year, we would run out of time in the school year—*Oops!*—and we would not be able to reach Vietnam. Some of us knew why, though. *We* knew why. We knew why never once was history taught in reverse, like it should be, so we got to know the times around us: it was a perfect world.

In the end, it didn't matter to us. We are all veterans, like Mr. Stuhby. We all inherited Vietnam. Such is how wars work. Some of us know it, like the students of Mr. Stuhby, and some of us don't. Such is how wars work.

Our minds raced trying to picture the wonderful card. We just couldn't, as much as we tried—we would have to wait for the real thing. It wasn't a real thing just yet. It would only be a real thing when it was a real thing, right there in our hands.

"Okay then," Mr. Stuhby said, smiling.

The next day, when Mr. Stuhby was to bring in his draft card, we were riding the bus to school as if it were any other day. Everything was still fine and normal on the yellow school bus with the black lines and black letters—after all, they made the school bus, all school buses, yellow with black lines and black letters on purpose—black and yellow is the color combination most striking to the human eye, most noticeable. So we children were protected.

In our yellow and black school bus we wound along the usual serpentine path, through a couple of neighborhoods, stair-stepping around the blocks, then along a straight, broad street for a few minutes without stopping, then delving down into another neighborhood, zigzagging along to scoop up more children. We looked out the windows and recognized every detail of the path, anticipated every turn.

At last we emerged from the last neighborhood out onto a busy four-lane drive, two lanes whizzing in either direction. The school was on this street, set back a safe distance from the road, behind a mown green lawn and the flag on a long skinny white metal pole. It was the home stretch, then, in five more minutes we would be there.

But a funny thing happened. We all remember it now, though it was forgotten for many years. Thinking of these times, it comes back somehow. *Vietnam.*

A siren started wailing. Otherworldly-bright blue lights, bright even during daylight, started flashing behind us. A cop was pulling us over. A cop pulling over a school bus at 7:50 in the morning.

We turned into the gravel parking lot of a dormant bar, its neon beer signs, squeezed into small black windows, now drained of their life-force, unanimated, hung over, worn the hell out. Sad gray ghosts looking out, caught behind small black windows.

The cop parked behind us and left his lights flashing when he exited the patrol car and we turned to look at that. We were silent. Then we heard the bus driver pull the crank handle which opened the door like it would for any kid, but there stood the cop. He was severely pissed off. He put one foot up on the first step and started yelling at the bus driver.

"GODDAMN IT what in the HELL do you think you're doing going eighty-goddamn-miles-an-hour down the road in a SCHOOL BUS loaded with CHILDREN!"

The bus driver, whose eyes were bulging out, stayed seated and looked down at the officer and tried to calm him.

"Officer, now, let's just — "

"— Let's just NOTHING! Are you shit-out-of-your-mind! What fucking business — the bus driver's eyes nervously flashed to the audience of bewildered children here, and several other times during the argument — do you have driving a goddamn school bus!"

"Officer, there are children — "

"I KNOW there are children which is why I cannot fucking believe you were doing EIGHTY down this goddamn road!"

The bus driver held his hands up in a calming motion. "Officer, could you please keep it down — "

"Jesus H. Christ! Keep it — "

"— the children, really there's no need to cuss — "

"— no need? Jesus fucking Christ! I'm gonna — "

"— *Please* officer, the kids — "

"— *Now* you're all concerned about the kids — you listen to me — you want to drive like an asshole, do it on your own time! I should just kick the shit out of you right here and now! You've got SHIT for — "

"— OFFICER!"

"Listen up! I am going to straighten you out! This is civilization! Here we — "

At last the bus driver stood and, in a voice the cop probably did not even hear over his yelling, suggested they discuss the matter outside. He stepped down and out of the bus and the cop continued railing on him as they went back to the patrol car and got inside, both in the front.

And it's a funny thing, but that's where our memory peters out, ends — if our bus driver drove us the rest of the way to school that day, we don't remember, or if he was there the next day, we don't remember, or if we ever saw him again, we don't remember. The memory, apparently, said all it wanted to say and went home.

In the classroom later that morning, the blackboard shone blackly in front of us, and Mr. Stuhby sat at his desk organizing papers. We were still unsettled from the strange bus ride to school. We were also looking forward to seeing the draft card, so our feelings were a mix of excitement and trepidation. We were nervous, but we only talked about the draft card, the card which Mr. Stuhby *promised* to bring in. Mr. Stuhby seemed to take his time.

Finally he stood before us and said, "Good morning." After a moment he said, "Today we're going to learn about Germany."

Germany! What about the draft card? He didn't *forget*, did he?

"Germany is actually two countries. But it's easy to remember. There's *East* Germany, and there's *West* Germany." He smiled and went over to the portable map and showed us where these things were. Then we methodically opened our texts to page one-ninety-four, where we took turns reading details of the place which made it seem only slightly more believable. For us to take it seriously we would need proof. Proof that it was real. Like we needed to see the draft card to truly believe in Vietnam. Because Mr. Stuhby, despite all of his wonderful characteristics, was not proof. People aren't proof. They're too changeable. Things are proof. The things of people.

So we learned all about the Germanys, anxiously hoping that there would be time left in the class for Mr. Stuhby to show us his draft card, if he had remembered to bring it. East Germany, West Germany. Heavy industry. Berlin Wall. Airlift. Et cetera. Finally Mr. Stuhby said, "That's enough for today. We'll talk some more about East and West Germany next week. Does anybody have any questions?"

We were silent.

"All right then, that should— "

What about yesterday? we blurted out. Mr. Stuhby looked confused, through a grin. "Yesterday?"

Yeah, we said, all chiming in with different voices, different phrases. You know, you said you would, when we talked about, you know, Vietnam, you said you were there and stuff, you could bring in the draft card?

"Ah, yes of course," he said. "I didn't forget." His smile expanded. We were playing into his hands. "I have it right here."

We all breathed a sigh of relief.

Mr. Stuhby then pulled from his pants pocket his wallet, a smooth, worn black leather lump; it was like he had pulled a tumor out of his body. The blackboard muttered something vague. But it was meant to be heard, this muttering to itself.

Mr. Stuhby went to open the wallet and then suddenly hesitated. We were dying with anticipation. "Question," Mr. Stuhby said, holding his wallet up before him. "Does anybody here—does everybody here—know *why* you're here, in school?"

Of course we were all silent, our arms unraised. It was an absurd question. There was no *Why* to things, there just *was*. We went every day to school because we had to, it was just what was done. It was important because they said it was. We did what we were told and when we did it well, they treated us well, they flattered us and spoiled us. That was the system, it seemed like a good system, it put us in relation to them and made achievement possible, it gave us some monkey bars to climb and if we did so, we got a banana. What more could anybody ask for? How could anybody think to ask for more, or for something different from what *was*? It made no sense. It was a good system. It was the only system. The existence of the one system excluded the possibility of there being other systems. No two systems could occupy the same space, correct? And if one system was in place, it was there for a reason. Because it was truly the only one possible. Because it was best, it had won out long before our time. Because god goddamnit meant it to be so.

"Why are you here?" Mr. Stuhby repeated. Why? Well— what the—but—Mr.—are you?—come on—I mean, Mr. Stuhby! This makes no sense. Leave it alone already. It hurts our heads. There is a reason for being here? There is a reason for things? For *everything*?

"I'll tell you why you are here," he said. "You are here to be *educated*." To be *educated*. Another loaded word. Locked and loaded.

"What does that mean? Educated? It means knowing about the world. Not just countries, their names and how many people live in them, but what they are like. And not just people. Knowing about the world means knowing about nature, earth and plants and animals. It means knowing about mathematics. And science, and history. The world is full of things to know. It takes a long time to hear about it, that's why you go to school for twelve years. To be educated. So you can see what is around you. So you can under-stand what is going on around you. So you can enjoy things more. So you can change things if you don't like them."

Change? That was it. That was scary. There was a reason. Reasons were now attached to things. The reason for school was education. And a synonym for education was change. We would change, and then we would change the world.

Mr. Stuhby then opened his wallet. He slipped the draft card out, and held it up for a moment in front of us. We were frozen by the sight of it. Mr. Stuhby's magic wand.

Mr. Stuhby—don't misunderstand—we love Mr. Stuhby. We are very thankful to Mr. Stuhby. We have no idea where he is now.

We saw the card. It seemed real. As did everything else— almost. The world was almost real. Mistakes were almost made, people almost suffered. Reason almost didn't prevail at all times. Greed and hate and ignorance and abuse almost existed. Truth was almost not omnipresent, a basic element, carbon, oxygen. Compassion almost did not rule, sleeping. There was almost something to be done in the world. The world was almost real—it was almost unfinished.

Mr. Stuhby went over to the first row and slowly handed the draft card down to the first student, who sat with his mouth hanging open in suspense. Then the card flew around the room and alighted on each of us, and we awoke:

We touched it. It was real. Vietnam was real. The world was real.

We were real. Without knowing why. Why us?

But there it is. The blackboard was silent.

And that was how we were drafted into the world.

Du Thi Hoan

Pray

The day I screamed my birth cry
my father went to the battlefield.
He had time only to see me tossed and turned, crying.
From that day we heard nothing but silence
                    so my mother tells me.

At night
my grandmother would grope her way
to the roof. Looking to the sky,
                  she would pray
three chopsticks folded in her hands
                bowing
in the nine directions of the earth,
in the ten directions of the sky —
pleading for my father's safety.

My mother would say
                that it is late at night
when the angels ascend.
And so we hoped these laments
would be carried to the Pearl Emperor.

And then grandma died,
and my father still hadn't returned,
                only his face smiling
from a photo that fit into my palm.

Tonight,
the night flower blooms in silence,
a shadow falls
              from the roof terrace.
My mother
folds her hands and looks to the sky.

Angels,
if now you ascend,

    bend down and
take my mother's sighs.

Tomorrow
my brother turns seventeen
and bears his knapsack to the army.

Translated from the Vietnamese by
Ho Anh Thai and Wayne Karlin

Anh Dao Kolbe, "Hanoi-Dong Xuan Market Rice," photograph

DEBRA McCALL

Wild Blue

I
Small hands cup the fuselage of a 314 Clipper,
lift it three feet into the air, spiral its descent
onto a plush carpet runway.
The hands belong to my grandson.
At my feet, he lines up a fleet of his favorites —
an F-86 Sabrejet, a red-tipped B-17,
a bent-wing F-4. He raises the Sabrejet
above his head with one hand.
With the other, he engages an MIG.
A dogfight ensues. *Brrr, brrrr, brrrrr.*

II
Christmas morning, first light, 0630 hours.
Our mission — to rescue Captain Brownlee
whose plane was shot down
over enemy territory the night before.
In the F105 Thunderchief, I fly cover.
This is Red Lead, Tower, ready for take-off.
Roger, Red Lead, you're clear.
The flight formation heads east from Takhli
through a gray-webbed mist toward Vietnam.
As we approach the target zone, visibility clears.
The Jolly Green Giant hovers over a thick clump
of trees fifteen-hundred feet below.
Airman King descends into a silent dawn.
The jungle penetrator he straddles
disappears beneath the foliage.
The second orbit around the target zone
and enemy fire breaks out.
King's voice, on the radio in short jabs,
Ambush. Pull out, pull out.
The forward controller spots the enemy,
locks onto him. Smoke rockets fall.
His report on the radio seconds later,
Enemy position is 50 yards at twelve o'clock.
I respond with my full reserve,

drop six five-hundred-fifty pound bombs,
one-hundred-forty rounds of 20mm.
Hours collapse to minutes—
my body, precise in each maneuver.
Smoke mushrooms above the field below
as in a silent movie.
To this day I cannot remember
the flight back to home base.
My two-thousandth landing occurred
without incident so I know I followed
standard procedure, arrived in formation,
broke away at five-second interval,
sharp to the left, rolled out 180 degrees
and put my landing gear down.
That night in the flight log I penciled,
Rescue failed, Brownlee, King lost.
The next day, I removed their pictures
from the Gallery Squadron.

III
Brrr, brrrr, brrrrr.
My grandson mimics enemy fire.
I ride the wild blue of his eyes,
my mind hovering towards thoughts
of Brownlee's grandson, of Airman King's.
Turbulence. A quick drop in altitude,
my stomach left behind as I spin
above the ground, struggling
to get the nose up
and pull out.

WAYNE KARLIN

The Eye of the Nation

for Tran Van Thuy

Queues of jagged white rocks break through the soil here and there, the spine, the people say, of the dragon that sleeps under the village, protecting it. Vinh looks down at the cluster of thatched houses from the hill, pans the Bolex over it, looking for a shot. What are wanted, he knows, are not dragon bones but peasant-heroes with rifles slung over shoulders, hands on plows; old women who have given all their sons and daughters to the revolution, their faces carved to nobility by age and grief; young women smiling as they squat and carve punji stakes to skewer the American invaders or puppet troops. And so on. He is tired of all of it, too tired even to think why he is tired. It isn't that such people don't move him, still, after all these years. He's seen the price they pay. He knows their sincerity. A sharp, sour taste rises in his mouth. He's been feeling bilious, his stomach bloated. The villagers have fed them simply but well, one old grandmother even finding some soybean milk sweetened with sugar for him, a taste that brought him back to his childhood. But for weeks, before coming here, he'd eaten with the soldiers, and the young girls in the Youth Volunteer unit he'd been filming: nothing but manioc and tapioca from the little fields they'd cultivated in the Truong Son Mountains, sometimes nothing but roots. Maybe that's all that was bothering him. His stomach. But a vague image is flapping insistently in his mind, its very nebulousness making him feel more ill at ease. It focuses into a flag being waved atop a captured bunker, and then, yes, he does know what has been bothering him. He hates doing reenactments. Prides himself on being there. He is the eye of the nation, he's been told, and has come to believe that

*Michael L. Gray, photograph

64

those words describe what he wishes to be. Too many of the other correspondents relied only on reports, official communiqués, but he was always at the front, with the people doing the killing and dying. Everyone knew his combat footage was the best, only rarely re-staged. Yes. But it had been a significant victory and he had not been notified until afterwards, when the soldiers had already buried their comrades. So he'd gone to the scene, and placed the filthy, weary men here and there, like arrangements in a composition. Told them to run this way and that, as the sappers set off harmless explosions. There had been a beautiful young private whom he'd placed on top of the heap of bloody, riddled sandbags in front of which so many had fallen, and he'd instructed the boy to raise and wave the national flag triumphantly, though in the real battle the commissar had forgotten or misplaced the flag. No matter. It was all as formal and choreographed as a classic dance. He'd comforted himself with the thought that at least the soldiers he'd used had actually been in the fighting at that place. But then, weeks later, a sergeant had told him that the beautiful private had been a coward who'd refused to advance, pissed himself in terror. He told Vinh this as if the cameraman could take back film once it was exposed, had the power to change a vision that met so many needs, as if it wasn't too late to tell the truth. Now the image of that boy had been seen in movie theatres in Hanoi and all over the North, and in War Zone B, in the South also, flickering onto parachute silk backdrops set up in caves and tunnels. Sanctified now and forever by his, Vinh's, film.

Well, he thinks, and so what? At least the boy would be of some use now. He was a good-looking boy, and in war, Uncle Ho had said, even poetry must become a sword. It was a lovely thing to say. A nicely balanced dichotomy. No. He shakes his head, rejects his own cynicism. Maybe it is just gas. His sour gut. In the unit where he'd picked up his two escorts, May and Manh, there'd been a commissar who checked the size and amount of the men's turds after their bowel movements, to be sure that everyone ate equally, everyone ate small. In the spirit of egalitarianism, Manh had said to Vinh. Film that, cameraman. In war, even shit becomes a sword. Another memory intrudes: once, at a jungle hospital he'd filmed, the doctors had shot an elephant and they had all feasted until their stomachs bloated. Unable to carve through the hide, they'd slit the belly and a surgeon had gone into the interior of the animal and carved it out with his instruments. Left it hollow. A representation of an elephant. Real only to those who had never seen a true elephant.

He hears a noise, swings the camera around, catches Manh running up the hill towards the banyan tree where he is standing. Manh is wearing a peasant's black cotton shorts and shirt, un-armed. Vinh centers him in the lens, then sweeps right and left, wondering where May is. His two guardians. He usually prefers to go on assignments alone, and he is valued enough now that headquarters lets him. But when he'd asked to do this assignment, filming Liberation Front villages and fighters operating right under the noses of the Americans in Quang Tri, headquarters had as-signed two liaison scouts to accompany him. He doesn't mind. They are repatriated Southerners and know the area, the people. May is a village boy who has somehow maintained a sweet naivety through five years of war, though his name, which means "lucky," sent a chill through Vinh when he first heard it: it is a name like a target, a name in a bad war film given the character everybody knows will die. Who in their right mind, in wartime, would name a child "Lucky"? Manh, standing in front of him now, reaching out a thin, fine hand to push the camera lens down, is the Sardonic Jokester. He'd been an art student in Hue during the anti-Diem Buddhist riots, had fled North after the massacre of students and monks. His home village is near here.

And he is, Vinh sees, very agitated.

"What is it?"

"Please come quickly. Don't you hear the helicopters? We've gotten intelligence that the Americans are going to sweep through here. Please, elder brother, put the camera down." Vinh has raised the lens to capture Manh's face, his eyes, at the moment he brings the news.

"How long . . . ?" Vinh begins, but as if his words have called it, he hears, at a distance, the sound of helicopter rotors beating the air. His blood freezes. An image — locusts eating his flesh — opens in his mind, it always does when he knows the helicopters are coming. They are the insects of insanity.

The dawn light makes the CH46 helicopters look like a neatly lined platoon of sinister grasshoppers. Ready to jump on com-mand. John wonders if they know who commands. Or care. He stares at the row of CH46's, sips at his coffee and lets his mind wander with the sun's rise. The hot metal cup stings the small cuts in his greasy hands: a few moments before, he'd finished struggling the heavy .50's into the armatures set behind the open front ports of the Sea Knight. He enjoys the feel of heavy metal slipping smoothly into position, hates to feel the sweat start and spoil the long cooling of the night.

He looks at Sam, up on the green back of number seven, peering at the engine. The barrels of both guns stick out of the side ports, perpendicular to the plane.

The pilots begin spilling out of the briefing tent. John gulps down the rest of his coffee and runs out to the helicopter. Sam climbs down and stands besides him, wiping his hands on his hips. They wait for the officers. Lieutenant DeLeon is walking slightly in front, his flight bag slapping against his legs. The co-pilot, a chubby new second lieutenant named Anderson, scurries to keep up with him. John stares at the handlebar mustache DeLeon has cultivated over the last month, wondering what picture of himself the pilot feels it completes.

Anderson climbs up to begin the pre-flight, while DeLeon briefs them.

"Sir, you said somethin' 'bout goin' to the 'Z again? Yester-day?" Sam asks.

"'Fraid so, Corporal Deeson," DeLeon says, smiling. "We have an extract up there. A recon team."

John is staring at the lieutenant's face. The sickness he's been feeling all morning is bursting in strong bubbles in his stom-ach. The face seems to him strangely translucent, almost gaseous behind the solidity of the mustache, as if only the anchors of the hairs are keeping it from blowing away. The lips in the face are moving, silent and rubbery, and John watches them in sick fasci-nation, not hearing the words coming out. He is sweating heavily, feeling the sweat spread over his skin like a dirty film of soot. Phu Bai, the lieutenant says. Dong Ha, DeLeon says, his voice coming from a distance. They look like nylon, those mustache hairs, John thinks, like each nylon hair filament is glued separately into each gaping little pore above the officer's lip. He can feel the soft weight of the nylon hairs encircling his skin and webbing him to the lieutenant. He feels lifeless, a small particle carried helplessly on DeLeon's words. He sees the lips moving and notices dully the ridge of yellow, cottage-cheesy material between the gums and the teeth. More teeth show suddenly as DeLeon grins. Keep your eyes sharp, he is saying. We'll be passing over some of those fucking villages, and if we get any of that fire we've been getting, don't wait for my permission to return it. It's a free fire zone. Do it. Waste them. Don't worry 'bout women and kids. Littledinksgrowinto - bigcong. Use those fifties.

Must come with pubic hair, this cong.

John watches DeLeon climb into the helicopter. He still feels detached from the entire scene, somewhere beneath it.

He follows Manh at a run, back to the village. They should keep going, get out into the paddies and jungle, Vinh thinks. But he defers to Manh. May is waiting for them behind Mrs. Ninh's house. "Quickly, elder brother," he says, his forehead wrinkled with tension at the responsibility he feels about Vinh. He leads them to a row of cactus fencing a small cornfield, grasps one of the cactus ears, and lifts. A small section comes up: the plants are in a foot of soil over a bamboo trapdoor. Vinh sees that flame-retardant *trung quan* leaves have been woven to the underside of the trap. The hole is deep, but the space inside looks barely large enough for one person. Manh jumps in, gestures for him to follow. It isn't, Vinh sees, a tunnel, simply an opening in the earth, wider at the bottom than at the top. A grave. He stops, but May firmly presses his hands against his back and pushes him as Manh grabs his wrist and pulls. Vinh goes in heavily, on top of Manh, who grunts, expelling breath rich with fish sauce into Vinh's face. Vinh looks frantically back over his shoulder and sees May closing the trapdoor after himself like the lid of a coffin.

It is immediately pitch black. Over it, he can hear the beating of locust wings. His heart scrambles in his chest like a trapped animal. Like himself trapped in this hole. As if he is a heart. He can hear his own blood pulsing in his ears, the sound as loud and hollow as the wooden fish drum at the village pagoda. His draws his knees up to his chin, clasps his hands around them. May and Manh must be in the same position, though he can't see them. There's no room otherwise. The earthen walls push on him. The surrounding darkness itself has turned to hot, wet flesh and is pressing at every inch of his body, sealing his closed eyes. Over all of it is the terrible whirring noise of locusts, and now he can hear explosions, a crescendo of firing, the crackling of straw on fire, even the hum of bullets. The affairs of the earth continuing un-abated, heard from his grave. Or waiting for him outside his womb. Here, in the belly of the dragon. His clothing, the thin shirt and shorts, takes on a weight of its own, adding another layer he begins to find unbearable. The buttons on his chest feel red hot as they push into his skin, his waistband squeezes his painfully bloated stomach. He lets go of the camera, useless in this dark, and claws at the buttons, the cloth twisting around him, until somehow he has gotten his clothes off. Next to him, he can feel May and Manh doing the same. They are pressed together, flank to flank, like fish steaming in a pot, gasping, and he wonders if they will breathe all the air in this little space. Their breaths are already filling it; they must be by now breathing mostly carbon dioxide, he thinks. The heat and the closeness and airlessness are panic itself, but what he fears most is the blackness, pressing at his eyes, taking away that sense, so that he is blind. He can't stand the thought. He begins scrambling for the lid, trying to straighten his knees, stand, but May and Manh both grasp him, pull him down, hold him. Manh, he thinks it is Manh, is forcing something into his mouth, a hard wooden tube—bamboo. He sucks at it, drinks the smoke-tainted air as if it is mother's milk. He is in a kind of trance. Manh—or is it May?—slides the tube out of his mouth, the joints of the bamboo segments scraping his tongue, passes it to the other man. The third fetus, Vinh thinks dully, his brain heavy and soft and fibrous in his skull. The soul transmigrates into the body of the baby waiting to be born. Pressed into the womb, would the soul's past life reel past its inner eye in flashing images, frame after frame, fast forward, reverse? All the strips and squares of film seen and forgotten or left cut into strips in the jungle mud, the floor, would they be pasted back together for a final viewing? Would he be allowed to reincarnate or would he be sent to one of the lower hells? Wombed and tombed now, he knows the answer. He knows what he has seen and what he has refused to see. The dragon hisses his, Vinh's, own secrets into his ears. He knows he is bloated with lies. He is the eye of the nation and he has chosen to be blind. He has allowed his eyes to create lies. The images the fetus plays on the screen of its interior vision are the price of lies. The lies are here with him now, in the dark, stinking and rotting, stillborn, they are his twin brothers, embracing him. What does he see? He had once seen and captured the long-suffering nobility of that old woman's face, her hands work-callused and capable, her life a paean to self-sacrifice. But he had closed his eye, capped his lens when it began to open a soul so battered with grief it had shrunken cowering into a small corner of the woman's mind, screaming behind her blank eyes, the stoic mask of her face. He had stopped filming, had stopped seeing, but now he sees the wreck of her daughter's body, flesh hanging in strips as if it has turned to paper, and the heap of bodies he saw and refused to see in Tay Ninh, a pile into which her sons might have been incorporated, Vietnamese and Americans, naked and entangled as lovers, as more than lovers, since so many of the parts themselves were separated and mixed, brown arm growing from white neck, white leg over brown chest, as if Heaven had torn this flesh in a rage, presented it, said begin again. Reincarnate. He tries again to rise, but his twins clasp him, hold him down tightly to themselves, in his pool of blindness, and outside fusillades of shots and screams and explosions that tremble the flesh of the earth and move into him, but he doesn't care, he just wants to push out of the blindness he knows now he has chosen for himself, he needs to see.

John peers through the port. The barrel of his machine gun bisects a piece of blue sky, hangs threateningly over the landscape framed by his window. The country north of Hue has broken out in thousands of Vietnamese grave mounds. The helicopter flies over stretches of sand and graves, then changes course further inland, where the country becomes shining brown mirrors of paddyland. The helicopter's shadow covers then uncovers some cone-hatted farmers. They don't look up.

John relaxes, feeling sleepy, but methodically, automatically scanning the country below now. He divides the area passing beneath him into segments, then, beginning at the front of the helicopter, scans each segment in turn. He is almost unaware of what he is doing, the slow, lazy routine of watching reducing everything to technique. The helicopter drones; he is a functioning part of the drone.

He shifts his line of sight back to the front of the helicopter and his complacency leaves him. A village is moving towards them. John sees it that way, as if he is suspended in time and space and the village attached to some moving assembly-line strip of

ground that is drawing under him. For adjustment. Green cauli-
flower trees and brown huts making an island in the mirror-
expanse of the paddies. A line of Marines moving off from it. Some
hooches burning at the edge, and in the center. A dead water
buffalo near a line of cactus. Not his ship's mission—a show he can
watch from his balcony. The war movie. He leans forward to get a
closer look as DeLeon brings the helicopter down to tree-top level.
The maneuver is supposed to confuse oriental snipers, the high-
tech roar of the engine startling them, and the helicopter gone
before they can get it together.

The helicopter is moving fast, maybe a hundred knots, yet
John's gaze falls and wraps itself around the doorway of one hut.
For a suspended moment he can see the doorway as clear and as
still as if he is walking up to it on the ground. The brown-yellow
thatch, untouched by the flames at the village's edge, stands out
starkly against the green around it, the contrast making it seem
more solid and substantial.

He feels a sharp twinge of connection with the hut, its
solidity filling the hollowness of his sickness. A woman is squatting on her heels in front of the door, absorbed in mixing something in a bowl. Ignoring the war. John imagines he can see her
betel-nut-blackened teeth smiling at the naked child playing next
to her in the yellow dirt, as if the soldiers who had gone through
had already passed into her history.

They are passing over the village and the passage tears at
him. He feels their transience in that moment. They are just a
loud noise and a green flash in the sky, gone too soon to be re-
marked upon. Their loudness is only, after all, a child's cry to be
noticed, a child's threat if ignored.

A string of tracers flashes up from a clump of trees just
outside the village.

May and Manh hold him down. He thinks he passes out
though it is hard for him to judge. In the close darkness all lines
and borders are invisible. He dreams the taste of sweet soybean
milk in his mouth. He is back in his boyhood home. In the courtyard some ylang-ylang trees stand near the well and a pile of red
tiles. He is walking Black Dog. As he walks, he thinks of a film he
will shoot about Black Dog. He knows in the film Black Dog will
run into a thicket and squat like a frog. He releases the dog

knowing it will follow his vision. Instead, it shoots off in the opposite direction, towards a brown and white heap of something on the other side of the courtyard. It is a dead cow. Black Dog clamps the cow's ear between his teeth, growling in his throat, and begins gnawing at it. He pulls the dog away, screaming, "It's dead!" They walk on and suddenly there is a tiger lying on the side of the road. He is confused. It shouldn't be here. There is no tiger in his film. It gets up, bares its fangs, growls, and Black Dog leaps towards it. Someone is shaking his shoulder. "Elder brother, wake up," he hears Manh whispering in his ear, and he feels the segmented bamboo being pushed into his mouth again.

He remembers hiding like this once before, huddled in a tunnel, almost caught when an American unit had taken over a village where he'd been filming. When the shelling and firing had stopped, he'd peered out of the earth, and in front of him, seen through a lattice of cactus, had been an American. His back was to Vinh. He had hung a small mirror from a peg on the corner post of a house and was shaving. Vinh had thought: have I been under-ground so long this has become America? He could see a small image of the man's face, lathered, in the mirror. There had been a bamboo table in front of him; on it, Vinh saw as the man moved to the side, was an upside-down helmet into which he dipped the razor. The American's back was covered with brown spots and here and there, patches of coarse hair. He seemed to be conducting an orchestra. A madman, shaving among smoldering ruins, as if to create an order only he could control. Vinh had been close enough to touch the man's back.

But now he doesn't know how long they have been here. The sweat of their bodies has glued them into one flesh and into the flesh of the earth around them. In the darkness the dream clings to him longer than dreams should, staining into the air. He can't see. He is suddenly, again, very afraid: what if the darkness has taken his vision permanently? He and the two other men are gasping, and when he puts the bamboo into his mouth again, no matter how hard he sucks, nothing comes through. If they stay here, he under-stands, they will die. He rises a little and pushes gently against the underside of the trapdoor, peers out of the crack he's made.

He drinks in the air. The light stabs his eyes. He closes them, opens them a crack also, like the door. Like the slowly opening iris of a lens. The world of the living slowly sorts itself out for him. To his left, a house. To his right, a dead water buffalo, on its back, its head twisted towards him, its fly-crusted eyes looking at him reproachfully.

He closes the lid. May or Manh is pulling him, clutching him, whispering to be cautious. But he has to get out. The hole now seems to be squeezing in on him, pulsing. He grabs his camera with one hand, pushes the lid up and over, opening the opposite side, just a crack. He slides through silently, keeping his chest and belly on the earth, keeping behind the cactus fence, then helps May and Manh. As each face peers at the crack, Vinh puts a finger to his lips. The three men lie on the ground. There is no wind and the stench of the fire and the dead buffalo is still thick in the air.

Manh begins crawling towards the ditch at the end of the cactus row. Vinh sees what he has in mind—the ditch runs to a field of elephant grass. If they can make that, they can get into the forest. He hears the noise of rotors.

"Gunner, didn't you see that fire?" asks DeLeon's voice in his helmet. "We have some reported movement down there." John doesn't answer. They are drawing out of range. "I'm going around," the pilot's voice insists; "let's take care of those people."

He looks at the cord connecting him to the cockpit, to DeLeon, a hair, a thing of flesh making him a functioning part of the pilot. The hollow-sick feeling returns and wells, spills from his pores, dirties him. Gunner, the Voice in his ears says, you have the first shot. The village draws under the helicopter. There is no firing from below now. Somebody is probably getting hell for opening up on the helicopter. Getting hell and he is the deliveryman. He points the barrel of the machine gun a little below and to the left of the area he wants to hit. Like training, he thinks. There is nobody in front of the doorway now. His fingers touch the butterfly trigger, a butterfly touch. He hesitates. Sam is watching him.

Vinh freezes, feels hot spots burn on his back and neck like premonitions of bullets. Hears a burst of firing, sees rounds flying up at the aircraft from the other side of the village. Perhaps to distract the aircraft from him. The famous guest, he thinks. Angry and sickeningly grateful at once.

The three men leap to their feet and run into the jungle. Like three red-assed monkeys, May will say later. An amboyna tree explodes into splinters not fifty yards away from Vinh. The rounds crash down behind him, and May groans a little as a splinter of wood slices his thigh. The earth is shaking under Vinh's feet as he runs. Suddenly, on his right, the forest disappears in a maelstrom. He is assailed by a great wind and noise, a slap of fire. He flies through the air, lands, rolls, runs on. He looks down, sees he is intact, though bleeding from what seem a thousand cuts.

There is a lull now. A great silence descends. The forest itself seems shocked and somehow pale. He sees the lens of the camera is shattered. Yes. It is what he deserves. His brain seems shattered also. Like a mirror. He sees the reflecting shards of it, a thousand fractured images, all gone. He picks the camera up like a broken child killed for his sins. Bad karma from bad actions. He remembers now what had run through his mind as he was embraced by the walls of that hole. The omissions of his past life. He was the eye of the nation and he refused to see. Now each image he had refused to press into the eyes of those for whom he was seeing lies imprinted on a shard of the shattered lens. They cut into his brain. It was right. His camera was a weapon and, in war, poetry must become a sword. But his camera was the eye of the nation and he should have pointed it at that political commissar in Quang Tri who checked the turds of the men in his company to make sure no one was eating too much, an image as true of the war as the men who had run without hesitating into enemy machine-gun fire from that outpost near Dong Ha, and truer than what he'd done to them afterwards, when he'd made them mere extras in a flag-waving, piss-pants lie. Yes, he thinks, dizzily, it is right now his lens is cracked, but he refuses to let go of the camera and Manh is shaking him and making him move.

What do you see, cameraman? The dragon asks him.

He sees a grouping of ylang-ylang trees in a small cool courtyard, an unexpected tiger lying next to them.

He sees three small naked men hunted by the terrible machines and armies of a Giant so large he can't see what is in front of him, under his nose.

He sees the hairy back of a beast who is peering into a mirror, so intent on its own face, it can't see what is right behind it.

He sees, when he looks closely enough, under the patches of beast hair, the vulnerable, freckled skin of humanity.

He sees again, the film running fast, jerking insanely, every death of body or soul away from which he has turned his camera, his sight.

"It's all right, elder brother, there, there," May says gently. "Don't you know my name means lucky?"

The green locust of the helicopter whizzes by overhead and he points his shattered camera up and in it captures, as if through the thousand-faceted eyes of a bee, the equally insectoid face of the American framed in the hatchway, peering blindly down through the dark lenses that cover his eyes.

Anh Dao Kolbe, "Incense Offer," photograph

After

GAIL HOSKING GILBERG

On the Way to DaNang

On the hairpin turns of Hoi Van Pass
someone tells me there are no such things
as syllables in Vietnamese, and to be sure
to notice the leper colony over there
in the mountains above the South China Sea.
Nothing at all gives away the war, not
the endless varieties of green, the rice paddies
off to our right, or the windy pine trees
that might as well be California.

The Marines arrived on Red Beach in 1965
and stayed until the end of the war,
somewhere north of Happy Valley and
GI Plateau. The only piece left the stone walls
of a PX and its foundation pillars like the forts
I created as a child outside my father's army base
in Europe. A woman as old as the war
carries a pole with bags of bread hanging from
either end, her head topped with a cone-shaped hat,
her clothes the same black pajamas my father wore
sitting on our living room floor in southern Illinois.

Elvis in Hanoi Twenty-eight Years after the War

In Hanoi when I try to buy
Two bootleg Elvis CDs
With American money, the owner
Shakes his head *no*.
Half of his arm is gone.

In the narrow space between two rows
Of music, discs slipped into sleeves,
He offers me a small red plastic stool.
My sister hands me *dong*
As we calculate the exchange.

I want to tell him about my father
Whose footprints disappeared
By a river in the south, but
There is no fight left anymore.

We two strangers have found
The vanishing point:
Currency, Elvis, this red stool for resting.

MARTIN OTT

Nick's Place

Dysfunction Junction. That's what we call the bar nestled
among a stand of trembling aspens on the county road linking
Yellowstone and Grand Teton national parks. The road's number is
not important. It's a two-lane of beaten asphalt that looks older
than it really is—with potholes for acne, skid marks for crow's eyes
and a shoulder no wider than a farmer's hamhocks. You've either
navigated this road on your way to college, or thought it was
quaint on a rustic trip to the country, or memorized every cranny
as you've ridden it back and forth to a town barely large enough
for its own post office.

Sometimes the road's driving you. Harder. Faster. The hum
of tires spinning into infinity. Occasionally, you slow below the
posted speed limit and note the words "Dysfunction Junction" on
the back of a deer-crossing sign. Most of us at the bar figure the
road marker was penned by Nick, old cougar that he was, marking
his turf.

Nick the joker. Nick the quick. The scent of him is still all
over his place. He built the L-shaped building that houses the bar
with his own hands during the summer of '71 after his second tour
in Nam. Everything—from the off-key piano in the bar's back
room to the taped-up dog tags dangling on a nail above top-shelf
whiskeys—reminds us of him. Even the park rangers from
Yellowstone and Teton. We can't look at their uniforms without
remembering how they're responsible, partially at least, for our
loss.

Sometimes, Nick's bar is better defined by what it lacks. He
doesn't allow hats because of the helmet he boiled in, following his
Captain through pocked hamlets and rice fields with a PRC-77
radio strapped to his back. He told us that staying close to the man
calling the shots was worth the added weight—a quarter of his
platoon fell in one battle alone. That also explains his ban on
radios. The gurgle of static, he told us soon after his return, will
drive any man nuts.

The real name of Dysfunction Junction is Nick's Place, but
no one calls it that. Not since the incident that put our hangout on
the map. At least, it made quite a splash in the local press: *The Cody*

Chronicle, The Thermopolis Tribune, The Sheridan Star. One of the tabloids even sent a paparazzo to hound us. But we knew how to get rid of that fast-talking slicker, just as we do anyone who crosses us.

We aren't vindictive, but this bar means a lot to us. To some, it is family—or as close as we'll ever come to it. And like in any family, there are rules and there are rules destined to be broken. And then there's the 17th parallel of rules, an action that carries irrevocable consequences. This particular line in the sand was crossed by the rangers earlier that summer during one of the worst heat waves on record. It was mid-July, mid-afternoon, mid-bender for some of us. The sulfur stench from the hot springs and geysers clung to the scorched grass outside like a second layer of skin. Tourists crawled across the hillsides like fire ants at a picnic, like the thousands of Oglala Sioux and Cheyenne braves who'd smothered Custer at nearby Bighorn.

A burly park ranger named Chris started the trouble by resting a whiskey and soda on top of the scratched piano in the back. He was just about to take his eight-ball shot in a loud game of doubles between the Teton and Yellowstone rangers at the bar's seldom-used pool table. Nick's older brother Gus—who bartends five nights out of seven—exploded when he saw the pint glass sweating on his brother's prized piano. He swore a blue streak across the tavern. Chris told him to stuff it. Gus barreled out beneath the serving station, snatched the cue out of Chris's hands and started hacking away at the rangers milling in the back, a half-dozen in all, two of them women.

Then the rangers attacked and the regulars pummeled back and there were fists flying, bones cracking, skin ripping, blood spurting, shrieks and shouts and curses. Cubby—a long-time Hollywood bit actor who'd moved to the area a few years back—hid behind his stool, protecting his vaguely familiar good looks. Sweet, a suburban housewife turned trucker, pitched a ranger woman through a window into the garbage-cluttered side lot. Hans smashed a bottle of Jim Beam over a Teton head and Sarah did her version of a flamenco dance on the rib cage of a Yellowstone ranger that Dave and Leo had felled. Finally, we routed the uniforms and threw them the hell out of Nick's, with Gus screaming and swinging and promising worse if they ever showed their faces again.

We went back inside and nursed our wounds, waiting for something, Nick's unlikely return perhaps. Those of us who've set down roots at Dysfunction Junction understand the false allure of traveling to the coasts for fame, love, and fortune. We know everything important in the world has already been discovered and forgotten. So we bide our time in the crannies of the nation's park lands, waiting for the awe and wonder we felt as children to return. We aren't sure whether it will open up like the glitter of a rare rock formation in a newly discovered cavern or the fleeting nighttime blooms on a desert cactus. We just believe in the possibilities and each other—and for most of us that's enough.

✿   ✿   ✿

The real story behind our attack on the rangers began a lifetime ago, or at least it must have seemed that way to Nick. He was a sturdy, good-natured kid growing up, the kind guys would pat on the back and women on the ass. But when he came back from Nam, some of the fire had gone from his eyes. What was left was a black wound in the center of his head, a slow smoldering, more coal than eyes, and we had no idea at first what might erupt from the depths of them . . . or him.

Before his tours, Nick had plans of leaving the woodland paths and stony fissures and boiled-egg musk of the geysers and traveling to New York, Europe, Japan. For art. For women. For adventure.

But after he came back, we never heard him mention these flights of fancy again, his face becoming as somber as the stone mugs on Rushmore. So Nick made himself useful by building his bar and watching over the drunks like a night patrol commander over rice paddies. Only we were the ones becoming soaked, over-ripened, spoiling on the vine.

Nick's vigilance never wavered. He kept himself to one drink a night, a tall shot of whiskey just before closing time. We could set our watches by it. And so life went. A lot of drinking, a little farming, the occasional odd job, the people in these parts came and went. Nothing changed much. Until the day she came through the door.

Her name was Jen, that's what she called herself, but the name her tribe gave her was Gentle Hands. Or so she said. We were used to people shading their pasts as they wandered through haunted park land that made idols out of murderers, collapsing landmarks, even the starving animals that ranged it. Depending on her stories and how much she'd drunk, Jen was half Oglala Sioux or Cheyenne or Crow. The other half must have been pure devil, no smoldering in that one.

We joked that she and Nick were both veterans, he from Nam and she—her battlefield was inside of her. Unlike us, whose wounds were buried inside livers, kidneys, and lungs, Jen carried her pain like a match against the flint. Anger spewed out of her mouth like ashes and brimstone. Face like a statue, mouth like a gutter. She could tickle those ivories, though. She'd come in plowed and plunk herself down behind the piano. We'd belt out songs and get blasted, the wood walls breathing and pulsing from the life pumping inside of them. We lost ourselves in joy for a while, reveling in Nick's happiness and Jen's lust. But like all good times, they weren't destined to last.

Nick was crazy about Jen. Hell, we all were. But she did everything a little too fast, lived a little too hard. To us drunks, whose centers of gravity made us more grounded and attached to our bar stools, it was obvious she was an addict. The signs weren't hard to spot, but Nick took a swing at anyone who bad-mouthed her.

He was going to ask her to marry him, or so he confided to us, his long-faced troops. She was always saying how she wanted to run her body over America: the mountains, the rivers, the city streets, from plateaus to gutters. She wanted to spread herself over every curve of it and he promised he would help her. His long-forgotten itchiness for adventure took hold of him like a fever.

Uncharacteristically drunk one night, he confided that he was going to pop the question at the top of the Empire State Building, the tallest skyscraper in the world. None of us had the heart to tell him it wasn't the biggest any more.

So we gave them a going-away party on a night when the moon hung low and yellow in the sky like a urinal cake. Jen was hammered and said we'd celebrate enough that night to make up for the rest of the summer they'd be gone. She was right, too. Jen and Nick didn't leave until almost sun-up, promising they'd just go a little ways and grab some shut-eye before heading on.

It was about a week later when the strange sightings started. Nick had gotten himself a Winnebago the color of a chestnut roan and personalized plates—JENNICK, a combination of their names. A soldering of letters that made about as much sense to us as how the rain and land joined together, transforming seeds into sprouts and sand into stone. A seamless joining that promised eternity—like co-mingled Native and settler blood seeped into red rock long ago.

People kept saying they saw this Winnebago rumbling around the park land, sometimes in Montana, other times in Idaho, South Dakota, too. We thought it was funny, like a prairie ghost story or the Mystery Van from Scooby Doo.

Until we saw it with our own eyes.

It was closing time, late July, the biggest moon we ever saw. Gus kicked us out at closing time and we stayed outside awhile smoking and finishing up our beers. The Winnebago came weaving past us, throwing up gravel on the shoulder of the road. It was mud-splattered, dented and humming along on bald tires. The license plate looked as if someone had tried ripping it off the bumper with bare hands, JENNICK peeking out from the twisted frame.

None of us could think of a good reason why Nick would be back and not stop in, so we called the police and notified the park staff. It was one of the rangers that found them, too. Parked in Teton at a weekly campsite. We knew we shouldn't hold a grudge against them for doing their jobs, but whenever we saw them . . . all we could think about is what they discovered and how it changed our lives.

❖ ❖ ❖

Not long after our brawl with the rangers, on a summer afternoon that made even the shadows inside waver from the sun, they entered the bar and our lives with wide smiles and an absence of fear. Their names were Oscar and Izetta, although they went by Ozzie and Izzie like they were characters in a 50s sitcom or a Salinger novel.

They were college students, they said, from Omaha, but their eyes told a different tale. When Gus carded them, Ozzie was quick to show he was 21, while Izzie wandered absently to the piano, running her hands along the keys too lightly to trip the hammers.

"We're in a band," Ozzie said, looking at the red lettering we'd put above the door one night. "Dysfunction Junction," he said. "Now that's a great name for us." Ozzie looked at Izzie, who ignored him, then ordered a draft for them to share as though he feared her absence, like he followed her into the unisex john when she had to go.

Then there was the question of their car in the parking lot, a vintage Mustang that had known garages and suburbs its whole life before being driven hard along the Western trail by these souped-up kids.

When the car disappeared the next day, Ozzie said they'd sold it, although they had no more money afterwards than before, and we knew everyone in the area who might have bought it . . . and hadn't.

So Gus let them stay in the field behind the bar overgrown with weeds, stunted corn stalks, and wildflowers, like so many of the drifters who had come before. They camped there with barely a sound and when they weren't with us, we looked to see if there was movement inside, our imaginations soused and the shadows ripe from the bar's yellow glow.

The kids spent weeks with us, sounding flighty and upbeat, talking about their dreams, but we knew they saw something of themselves in our red eyes and scarred hands. They planted themselves on a pair of bar stools in the corner where Nick and Jen had once sat, and their past was poured out to us slowly, like a bottle of tequila trying to hide its worm. It was obvious—they were running from something, just like we all were.

✦   ✦   ✦

After finding Nick and Jen, Chris and his ranger pals had rolled into Dysfunction Junction with their customary swagger and a duty to tell us what had gone on. Apparently, one of the campers in Teton had complained about a smell coming out of the Winnebago. It rose up in the winds off the mesa bluffs and settled like a dark cloud over the site. The campers thought it might be a dead cat, but it wasn't . . . it was Jen.

She'd overdosed on smack the first night they left. That's what Chris told us after hemming and hawing, explaining how Nick had been pacing at the foot of her bed, anxious to keep them from touching her where she was laid out—his rotting angel. The rangers laughed at that and Gus kicked them out of the joint, telling them to never come back.

And as for Nick? No charges were filed against him. We can thank semi-regular Sheriff Pellson for that. He took the heroin and flushed it down the bar john soon after dropping Nick back in our midst. Nick was out of his mind. In grief. In anger. In a lightless prison that was his eyes. It was almost like we didn't know him. At first, we wondered if he might not have been using himself, but his arms were clean, his legs were clean.

Nick got hammered his first night back like we hadn't seen him do since he was a teenager. He kept talking crazy shit, about how he'd promised to let Jen rub her body over the yellow prairie bluffs and that he still wanted to ask her to marry him on top of the world's tallest building . . . a building made of ash.

She lay in a coffin over at Clark's funeral home in Cody. We never did know what tribe she was from or who was her nearest kin. Nick kept insisting we were her family and persuaded a couple of us to drive him over to see her—so he could pay his last respects. On the way, he cranked the radio and crooned over the staticky rock in a language seemingly without vowels.

Once we got there, he starting calling for Jen to come out. He scooped up gravel and flung it at the windows of the funeral home. At first, he was like a teenager trying to get his girlfriend's attention. Then the pebbles bounced harder on glass as he pitched them from behind the cover of his truck, and we ducked away from the rain of shrapnel. He ordered us to lower the bed of the pick-up so that we could take her with us.

He charged up the steps and kicked in the front door, all the while yelling for us to flank him, but we just couldn't. He wasn't quite able to get the coffin in the truck without our help. At the end, he laced his hands around his head in a helmet of flesh, and called out our coordinates for dust-off to the still-blaring radio.

The police came of course—hard not to with all the racket—and they took him away. He's in a home now, for people with problems accepting the way things are.

And it was then we knew that if the country had a heart, it was made of stone that sometimes cracked under the strain of great weights or boiled in underground geysers or turned to mush from the rain that had fallen through us.

❊   ❊   ❊

A couple months after the kids showed up, Ozzie and Izzie camped out at the bar on a night when a storm had turned them out of their leaky tent with gales and sputters and young hands to be warmed.

They had been avoiding us for a while, seeing the need in our eyes and too embarrassed for the charity we heaped on them. But that night they relented, and we bought rounds for the place one by one, getting everyone heated and squishy on the inside.

After a shot of rye ordered up by Sarah, Ozzie and Izzie moved to the piano. She played songs none of us had heard before and Ozzie played along with a mouth harp tuned to the wind whistling outside.

At first, we expected Gus to stop them, but he came back from behind the bar and pressed in the circle around them like the rest of us, leaving Sweet to dispense liquid cheer with her soft truck-driver's hands.

After a while, we learned the melodies and sang along like mountains breaking in two, bison rumbling across the plains in thundering herds, echoes of Native drums on the spine of the Black Hills.

We sang like there was no tomorrow and, of course, tomorrow came.

Just before midnight, a stranger slipped through the doors with a city accent, polished shoes, a worn suit and a bulge in his coat that told us everything we needed to know. He was a gun for hire, a dead-eyed detective.

Behind him followed a man who wore the grief of fatherhood as closely as the rain poncho that clung to his skin. "Izetta," he said to her, and she froze at the keyboard.

"And you," he growled at Oscar, "she's only sixteen."

And the private dick lurched toward Ozzie, who sidled away from the bench, but the sight of Sheriff Pellson at the bar stopped him and the P.I. both. What happened next is a matter of park lore.

The boy flew like the thirteenth blackbird or Thelma and Louise in perpetual drift across the Grand Canyon.

In three impossibly long running steps, Ozzie launched himself from the piano bench, flew over the pool table and the pitcher of Bud at Dave and Leo's table, and dove perfectly out the windows, whose fresh glass from the ranger incident shattered like thunder.

What happened next—the footsteps disappearing into the night, the father's tears as he clutched his baby, the water that flowed from the wound in the bar across the dusty floor—was like a cleansing, a cold draft piercing through us all.

Of course we had seen many crazy nights over the years, but this one came at us filled with joy, then grief, and all the weight of a slow-moving storm that would not abate. A few of the regulars cried after the kids were gone and the weaker ones clung to the stronger, and no one drank another drop, although it was an hour to closing.

❀ ❀ ❀

After that evening, the regulars erected a new sign for NICK'S PLACE atop the bar, then disbanded for a while. We went back home to make amends with scattered loved ones, long-shelved friends and estranged relatives. Gus even made a trip to visit Nick at the state home in Billings. It went well, we suppose. He spends fewer shifts at the bar. We know that Nick will return in time . . . but we have all the time in the world.

So we continue on with our small talk and our small lives in one of America's forgotten hollows, tucked away between jagged ridges and unending prairie. The sky's belly hangs so low we can pocket the clouds by day and harvest the stars at night. We never mention the incident again, just as we do not speak about the young couple that passed through. It doesn't take much in the way of brains to figure out they provided us with a wake . . . but one for the living, for Nick, for wounds eventually healing. Then again, if you think about it, wakes are always for the living, just as wars—even unpopular ones or those long forgotten—can bring the touch of death to gentle hands.

JUDITH CODY

Going Home

battlements razed

When enough time had elapsed
so that some of the soul
could be deposited back
into the coffer of the body
the body then cleansed, coiffured
contained in an unsullied
soldier suit, the old familiar
smile affixed to the sad face
the medals pinned upon the
anguished breast, only then
were the fathers
returned to their homes.

Old Têt Replays in the Third Millennium

California, 2002

Only the whirl
of thousands of blades slicing air like salami
like bullets burning holes in people
like screams slicing the air like bullets
like war bulletins slicing air like blades
like fear in our ears
like new ways to die
every new minute.

Like blades slicing their way to hospitals
like people sliced in surgery screaming
like leaves sliced from trees by tornadoes
like hell folded up like a paper plane flying
like spent bullets resting in brains
like spilled blood
like skin liquified by fire
like sliced soap.

Only the moans of thousands of people
bound to baskets bound to helicopters
bound to wards where burned soldiers are collected
like moths pinned to machines still alive,
like soldiers, like fathers, like lovers, like kids.

Only the whirl
of thousands of blades slicing my dreams
like screams, splattered guts, stinking burns
like the same roaring scene played over and over
on thousands of nights, even days, even when
cool silence calms memories, buries visions
like a simple traffic helicopter overhead
wakes the dead over and over.

ERIN MURPHY

My Father in Gray

gray like the carpet
in the black & white photo

where I'm an airplane
soaring on his feet

like the pencil lead
on the postal exam

that gives him extra points
for being a veteran

like the steamy jungle of
dreams he can't remember

in the morning, the pills
he says he doesn't need

the label on the vodka bottle
he keeps in the glovebox

gray like his only suit,
the one he wears

to every wedding and every
funeral, even his own

Elizabeth Keller Whitehurst

Pigs

Michael and I are into pigs. Big time. Some people save dogs, cats, children—we save the pigs. Now we didn't plan it this way. But my mama always said, "Don't you worry none, Wanda. The Good Lord will find you when he's got a job for you to do. He knows where you are."

Well, that's exactly what happened. Michael and I saw this ad in the paper for these potbellied pigs. We'd seen 'em racing at the fair and thought them real cute and all. Michael told me, "Honey, if you want one, we'll get you one." That's how good he is to me. Treats me like a queen. If I want it, I get it—within reason, of course.

Anyway, that's how Paddywack came into our lives. Shoot, we figured he'd just grow to be the size of a big dog—like a Lab. Never dreamed by the time he finished growing old Paddy would weigh over 200 pounds! The ones at the fair sure weren't that big. We loved him anyway. I know it's hard to believe just looking at me, but I actually weighed that much myself once upon a time.

When Michael asked Daddy if he could marry me (I guess since he was older he felt he had to) he said, "I love Wanda and I want to marry her and take care of her all my days."

And do you know what my daddy said? "Well, she's mighty fat." Honest. Those exact words popped right out of his mouth.

"Daddy!" I shrieked. Just like he'd slapped me.

"Well you are, Wanda."

"But it don't matter to me. No sir," Michael said.

So Daddy said yes and Mama cried and we got married at the First Brethren Church, reception in the Fellowship Hall—the whole shebang.

*James Tuong Nguyen, photograph

Let me tell you how we got into this pig business and started S.O.P.—Save Our Pigs. Now Michael, God love him, has some problems that weren't immediately apparent. Awful fierce flashbacks from his time in Vietnam. He almost goes crazy sometimes, thinking he's back there, halfway between asleep and awake. Only he can't wake up. Thunderstorms are not pretty—believe me. I'm happy to say he never abused alcohol or drugs, which is a miracle when you think about it.

Anyway, Michael took to this Paddywack like there was no tomorrow. Calmed Michael way down. He'd hug that pig, set him on his lap—before he got so big, that is. Just love up on him. "He's the son I never had," he likes to say. Which makes me feel real bad since we don't have any kids.

So we started saving to get us a place with more land. Paddywack needed it. And there was more to come. We have our neighbor, Diane, to thank for that. She does nails over at the mall. A real artist. She can airbrush like you wouldn't believe. Diane called me one evening after I got home from work. I work for Dr. Steward, an oncologist up at the hospital. "Could you and Michael use another pig?" Diane asked after I said hello. She knew how crazy we were about Paddywack. "We found this one that's mighty pitiful. Somebody's been hitting on it real bad. Can't hardly walk."

"Mercy," I said. "I'll talk with Michael and get back to you."

The next morning at breakfast, Michael sat at the table and said, "You know, Wanda. Everybody needs somebody. Even a pig. Let's take him."

We did. His back was real bad off. You could hardly bear to look at it. Now Michael's a big man, a full-time professional firefighter with the county. Believe me—he's tough. (I have to be the same way with my patients at the hospital. So many of them die.) Back to Michael. You wouldn't call him the sensitive type. But he took one look at that beat-up pig and lost it! Right in front of Diane.

We took the pig home and named him Poke-Poke and he's been with us ever since. At first he was so scared he'd drop right down onto the ground and squeal bloody murder if we'd come anywhere near him. There's no squeal like a pig's. But we spent lots of time with him every day after work. Paddy wasn't the least bit jealous. First Poke relaxed a tiny bit with me, but still couldn't bear for Michael to come near. Michael went out there twice a day and little by little Poke grew to love both of us, knew he could trust us.

Pigs are extremely intelligent. Why, the Farmer's Almanac had this article that listed them just below monkeys—but I think they might even be smarter than that. For instance, the pigs know when Michael's coming home. No. It's not the car they hear, because they get worked up way before he even starts driving down the road. And he comes home at different times every day. It's just weird.

So how did I get so thin? I guess you're wondering. Hard work, let me tell you. And, about six months after the time we got Paddy—Poke hadn't come into our life yet—Michael was carving up this honey ham I'd made for supper. He stopped right there with the butcher knife held above the ham (I'd cooked it real fancy with pineapple rings and cloves). "Wanda, honey. I know you worked real hard on this lovely ham, but, really—what difference is there between this here ham and our Paddy?" Then he dropped the knife on the counter, ran to the bathroom and threw up. Since then we've been strict vegetarians. I tell you, these pigs have changed our lives.

After we took in poor Poke-Poke, the word got around the county and before we knew it we were getting calls galore. Now we're up to 220 pigs. Uh-huh. We spent all our savings and bought us an 18-acre farm. We've got pens, stables, yards, even a little mud pond. Oh, don't they love that!

And let me tell you, if you want a window into the mysteries of the human soul—look at how bad people mistreat pigs. We got Casey—attacked by some pitbull, left to die in a ditch; Yoda—kicked out of a petting zoo because he couldn't take it when kids poked him with sticks. Then poor Chi-Chi, with one ear and a scar the length of his body. Oh yeah, someone tried to skin him alive when he was a piglet. We've had pigs crippled because they've never had their hooves trimmed, pigs with broken legs never set and healed crooked, beaten with 2 by 4's and their backs nearly broke, cigarette burns, words carved into their flesh. Poor Rudy can't stand up at all so Michael's rigged a wheelchair for him. This is what we're dealing with. Sometimes people just don't want their pig anymore and give him to us. But this is rare. Most all our pigs have been damaged in some way. Our biggest is Big Earl at 800 pounds. Yes! That's big even for a farm pig.

It's our life. We used to just sit around after work—drinking beer, eating chips, watching TV. I used to tape my soaps and watch them at night. Michael got wrapped up in them, too. He'd either be watching with me or else he'd just sit on the screened porch in the dark and stare out to the road. I hated those staring times most. Sometimes he'd sit so still he'd scare me. But now we don't have time for any of that. The pigs depend on us.

"You know, Wanda," Michael always says. "These pigs are not our pets. No, ma'am. We are all equals here."

He works so hard and gets so tired. He's up at 3:30 every morning—rain, snow or shine—feeding them. He talks to each one personally. "Hello, Mr. Oinks. Hello, Chestnut. Hey there, Sally." Each pig has his or her own name and personality and Michael and I know them all.

I'll sleep in until 4:30, then get up and go finish feeding them with Michael until I have to go into the hospital. Work an eight-hour day, at least, we're crazy busy in that office, then home to Michael and the pigs. We hardly have time to eat ourselves be-cause we've got to do it all over again at night. Might not get into bed 'til midnight. The simple fact is there's a real need to help these animals, as Michael says. Plus it's so good for him. That's why we do what we do.

Now I will tell you something about Michael. He never talks about ""Nam," as he calls it. I know though—he did some bad things. I've seen many movies on this subject. I think his sergeant or whatever probably told him to do it. You have no choice then. But I know Michael. That wouldn't count as an excuse to him. It hurt him real bad doing these things. When I try to get him to talk about it—you know how good they say talking is—he just shakes his head and says, "Some things are best forgot."

Besides the movies, I don't even know much about that war since I was just a baby when it was going on, but one thing I've noticed. Nobody who went there is right. It did something real bad to them. And it did it to Michael, too. I've seen the effects.

That's what I think about when I feel tired all day. Or won-der if they can smell pig shit on me at work. The smell is enough to knock you out. I try extra hard to be clean. Take a shower in the morning when I finish my chores. At night after feeding. But still I feel it's seeped into my pours, nostrils, hair. But those pigs are so good for Michael. I did it all for him. Until now.

She wakes me every night at 2 a.m. This voice just rises up and scares me half to death. No. It's not in my head. No way. It's outside of me. Loud and so clear. And every time I'm sure Michael, lying beside me spread-eagled on our king-size waterbed, snoring, is bound to hear. But so far, he just sleeps right through it.

I already called in and said I'd be late for work. "Thanks for meeting me, Diane," I say and she squeezes my hand, careful not to poke me with her long blue nails, each an airbrushed beach scene, palm trees and all. Like little worlds on each of her fingers.

We sit in the booth right across from each other. "Sure, honey. Now, what's up? Trouble in paradise?" Her low, cigarette voice is always so comforting. We order coffee.

"No. Well, yes. I don't know. Strange, Diane. Strange. You're like to think I'm crazy."

"Look, I've heard it all and then some. Come on now. Out with it. It'll make you feel better." She takes a big swig of coffee from her mug.

"It's just that every night for the past six nights in a row, I wake up at exactly 2 a.m. even though I'm dead tired."

"And?"

"And I hear this voice. I swear I do. It's a woman."

"Right there in the room with you?" Diane's eyes go wide. I nod.

Diane grips the table. "What does the voice say?"

"She says, 'Wanda, you've got to get the hell out of here.'"

"Oh, Lord," Diane says and shakes her head at the waitress who's just scurried over to refill our cups. Waits until she gets to the next table. "This might be a message from your guardian angel," she says with a completely straight face.

"You think?"

Diane nods several times. "It happens," she says. "Haven't you read any of those books about it? Watched the TV show with that good-looking Irish girl and Della Reese? Been on forever."

I shake my head no. "We don't have much time. You know, with the pigs."

Diane takes my hand. "How are you doing with all that?"

Suddenly, all the ugly thoughts I've had since the voice started come tumbling out. "Well, to be honest, I'm right tired after ten years of these pigs. I mean this is supposed to be the prime of my life—am I right?"

"Has it really been ten years? Don't seem possible. Honey, not to pry, but how much older is Michael than you?"

"Oh, twenty years."

Diane doesn't say anything for a minute, then slaps the table so some of our coffee sloshes out. She ignores it. "I know just what you need! A trip. Get away from it all. They've got these bus trips to Atlantic City. Honey, I've gone myself and it's a fabulous place, let me tell you. FAB-U-LOUS. All the food and drink you want for free—whether you gamble or not. I just love those slot machines.

"But you don't have to gamble. You and Michael could have yourself a real good time. I guarantee everything will look different when you get back!"

The idea plays across my brain for an instant but almost before Diane finishes telling me about it I blurt out, "Michael won't go. He'd never leave the pigs."

"Now wait just a minute. Don't give up so easy. Where there's a will, there's a way. Trust old Diane now. I bet there are some FFA members at the high school who'd love to make some extra money helping out. You wouldn't have to pay them that much. Now what do you think?"

"Maybe," I say.

"Look, honey. You need a lift. A little excitement in your life. That's what the message is—your guardian angel I mean. Everybody needs a little excitement. You and Michael could get away and, you know," she says and winks, "mix it up a little. It's always better away from home." She winks again, even bigger.

"Oh, no. No. Michael and I. Well . . ." I can't believe I've just told her this.

"What!"

"It was the war. Agent Orange. 'I've got some little boy troubles down there,' is how he explained it to me. He even had to have surgery. Of course he told me all this before we got married. But I was so happy he wanted me I couldn't let that stand in my way."

"So you don't . . . Oh, honey. Oh, you poor baby. So young, too." And I think Diane's going to cry right here in Bob Evans.

I glance at my watch. "Oh, gee. I've got to go."

"Didn't do anything. Don't mention it and run along. Coffee's on me," Diane says. "Think about that trip now."

When I glance back to wave goodbye I catch her shaking her head, tears still brimming in her eyes.

The voice doesn't let up. Every night at two on the dot she wakes me. Every morning at 4:30 I find it harder and harder to get up and out. To do my job feeding the pigs. Find I talk to them less. Never pet them, neither. Just go through the motions.

And, for some reason, I started counting the words Michael says to me every evening when we're finished with our chores. Pig talk doesn't count here. They are "Guess I'll turn in" and "goodnight" with a kiss on my cheek attached to it. When I realize he's said the exact same thing for seven nights in a row (and probably has been doing it the whole time I wasn't counting), I have to fight down this scream. Ugly, like an animal itself, it climbs right up my throat every time he gives me that goodnight kiss and turns his back to go on to bed. I'm afraid one night soon that scream might grow too strong to hold down.

I've also started crying at work. Every day. I just don't understand it. Before, I could be real professional. That's what all the doctors and nurses tell us in staff meetings. We have to be health professionals. What I think they mean is be real nice to the patients but don't feel anything. Because if you start to feel, even just a little bit, you'll be crying all day long.

Now, when I see the people pouring in for their chemo or radiation or whatever they're going to do to them, I look into their eyes. I can't resist—they're like magnets. And tears well up in mine every time. I keep acting like I've got a cold but that's not going to play much longer.

The other day, Angela, the chemotherapy specialist, happened to come up front for a patient's chart and caught me. She grabbed my arm. "You're okay, aren't you?" The way she said it was not a question. She may have meant it kindly but I'm not sure.

And I find I've been coming home to Michael later and later, picking up ready-made food at the Food Lion for our supper. Michael hasn't said anything, but I know he doesn't like it.

After Michael's goodnight kiss I fall into bed beside him as usual and at 2 a.m., as usual, the voice or guardian angel—whoever she is—says her thing. And I lie there, wide awake, stare at the ceiling for the longest time.

You won't believe what happened the other night. After the voice, I turned over in Michael's direction and with the moonlight shining into the room saw he was gone. I listened awhile for the toilet. No flush.

He wasn't in the house. I turned on the outside floodlights and saw the barn lights were on. I almost went on back to bed, but found myself wrapping my coat around me and padding out in my bedroom slippers, even though I knew the mud would ruin them by the time I got back.

I found him in the barn. At first I was afraid he'd passed out and almost called "Michael!" until I heard his telltale snore. There he was, sound asleep, overalls over his pajamas, lying down in the dirt with his arm draped over Big Earl. They both had the most peaceful smiles.

I just stood there watching them for the longest time, shaking from the cold night air. Feeling that scream scrambling around, fighting to come out.

Diane calls me at work the next day. "I've done a little research for you. Called Doug Denham, you all know him? He's the FFA advisor up at the high school. He says Ada Rose Kuntz and Lester Barlow were his two stars of FFA this year. And guess what? They know pigs! Both raised them and won ribbons at the fair last year. And they could use the money, too. Now what do you say?"

I feel so tired I could lay down on the nasty brown-speckled office carpeting and sleep for weeks. "I'll talk to Michael," I manage to say.

"You okay?"

"Just can't sleep."

"That angel still bothering you?"

"Uh-huh."

"Message changed any?"

"Nope," I say, trying to sound light. "Same."

"Oh. Well, I really think you should go for this trip. And honey, I've been meaning to say . . ."

"Gotta go right now, Diane. Thanks so much. Talk with you later."

When Michael comes in that night after his chores, hangs his flannel coat on the hook by the door, I'm waiting for him. I've cooked his favorite dinner—lots of macaroni and cheese, rolls, tossed salad, apple sauce, mixed fruit. All homemade.

We eat awhile in silence, then I say, "Michael, about the pigs."
His head jerks up, "Somebody sick?!"

"No, no. Nothing like that. They're all fine. It's just, I was
talking to Diane and she said we needed to get away—maybe go to
Atlantic City. Well, we wouldn't have to go there, we could go
anywhere, not that there's anything wrong with Atlantic City. . . ."
And all my practicing on the way home flies right out the window
and my mouth has a mind of its own. "And I was also thinking,
maybe we could try—well you know. I know you have your problem and surgery, but Diane says . . ."

Michael stares at me, his face grim. I so want to wipe off some
yellow macaroni juice that has splattered into his bristly mustache,
but don't. "Wanda, you didn't, you wouldn't dare mention my
problems to Diane."

I gasp. "No! Oh no. Of course not," I back-pedal. "Why she'd
tell everybody in the county." I giggle nervously. How could you? I
yell at myself. No sleep is no excuse for revealing deeply personal
details of your marriage. Neither is feeling so unsettled about
everything. No excuse at all! You're definitely losing it, I decide.

Then Michael gets this strange smile on his face, staring right
at me. He cocks his head. "Wanda. You've been reading some of
them magazines I see in the checkout line at the 7-Eleven. Maybe
watching that Dr. Phil? Aw, honey," he says and takes my hand.
"You don't have to worry about a thing. About pleasing me in that
way. It's a matter of discipline. Discipline, you see. That's what got
me through 'Nam. Got me back, too. They talked about discipline
all the time over there. Yep, it's the big D." He goes all quiet and
stares at the salt and pepper shakers.

That night, the angel's message is louder than ever, like she's
on some P.A. system.

The next day when I go down to lunch in the hospital cafeteria, I pass right by the salad bar, which has fed me ever since the
pigs entered our life. I calmly walk up to the sandwich line, feel my
heart beating too fast but also a new sensation—my mouth is
actually watering. "Lettuce and tomato, mayo, Swiss cheese and . . .
ham. On rye. Toasted." Say it like I've been saying it every day for
years. Eat the whole thing. Believe me—it's delicious.

Diane calls every day to check on me and fill me in on the

Atlantic City angle. "There's a trip Parks and Rec is sponsoring February 14th weekend. Get it? Valentine's Day! Celebrate with a trip, a big getaway! What do you think?"

"Michael said he'll think about it," I tell her, which is a lie. "You know we can't leave the pigs," he said in that "how could you have thought of such a thing" voice. But telling her what she wants to hear gets Diane off the phone. Besides, I have to go to the ladies room because I've been crying again.

This girl I graduated high school with was just in here. LeAnne Whitacre. She had her second chemo treatment first of the week—six hours' worth. She was in here bawling and screaming, "My hair! My hair!" so much the nurses had to take her into a consulting room. It was coming out in clumps in her hands. She'd pull a clump out and drop it on the floor. There was already a pile at her feet when I peeked in to see what all the noise was about. The nurses gave her a shot to calm her down. She'd already lost a ton of weight. I remember she used to wear the same size gym uniform I used to wear. Now she looks like she weighs about 100 pounds tops. Like one of those Holocaust people.

God. I wipe my eyes, try to rub the smeared mascara off. "Get a grip," I holler at the face in the mirror.

During the next week, I make me a list. Ever since I was a little bitty thing, lists always make me feel good and organized and powerful. So I write all the reasons for leaving (they always tell you to do this in magazines) and all the reasons for staying.

Reasons for going:

1. This is the prime of my life and I'm wasting it.

2. I'm still a virgin after 15 years of marriage.

3. The smell.

4. No sleep—either from the hard work or that damned angel voice.

5. Michael won't even miss me.

6. Meet new people. Do exciting things. Go to Atlantic City.

Reasons for staying:

1. Michael loves me.

2. Michael is good to me.

3. Michael needs me.

4. If I leave, I'll probably get fat again.

5. Where would I go?

I decide I've got to talk to Michael. That's exactly what Dear Abby would tell me to do. And I'm also thinking Michael suspects something's up. I catch him watching me a lot. And he's saying even less than usual.

That night he's not in the house when I get home so I go out looking for him. Find him in the barn with his gun over his shoulder. At first I figure some animal—a fox or something—must have gotten in. But he whips around and stares at me like a stranger. "I'm going to kill 'em," he screams. "I got these orders to kill 'em all. The devil's in 'em, I tell you. Just like in the Bible. Remember Jesus run them pigs into the Sea of Galilee? All our pigs got the devil in 'em now. Don't know how it happened. No choice. I gotta do it." He lifts the gun into the air and shoots it off, making me jump a mile.

"Michael." I can hardly speak, feel giddy.

He lunges over at me and grabs me by the shoulder, the gun coming close to my head, sticks his face in mine. "Even the little ones, honey, though I sorely hate to. It grieves my heart. But when you get an order, you got to follow it. Wanda, you have no choice. That's it."

I watch him pacing back and forth, working himself up to it. Then he cocks his gun, aiming right at Big Earl. All the pigs are squealing loud enough to raise the dead, smelling our fear, their danger. As he raises his gun, the scream stuck in my throat for so many months tricks me and cuts loose—echoing through the night—through the empty farm. Only Michael and I can hear it. Us and the pigs. It has a life outside of me and screams, "NO!" And then again, over and over, like a warning buzzer, "No! No! No!" And in the crazy slow motion of terror, I remember Mama always said, "You best be careful what you pray for."

But somehow I know exactly what to do. "Give me the gun, Michael," I say to him just as stern, with a power I've never felt my entire life, just as mean and commanding as any sergeant. "Michael, I mean it. Drop that gun. You don't have to kill Big Earl. Your orders were wrong. Ignore the orders. There's no devil in any of them pigs!"

He looks at me and I watch his legs buckle and he slowly falls to his knees, like all that bad energy has run its course and drained right out of him. The gun hangs down and I hear him click the safety lock into place.

I go over to him and he looks up. "I love the pigs, Wanda," he says.

"I know you do."

"I was just following orders."

"Yes, I know about that, too. I've been getting some orders of my own," I tell him.

"But you don't have to follow them."

"That's right. You don't. Not if you don't want."

"But how do you know? When to follow them and when not to?"

I watch him, shivering, feeling the weight of it all. Every one of those 220 pigs could be standing on my shoulders, Big Earl included. "Oh, Michael, I've got to tell you," I say, shake my head, stare out the barn door into the night. "I just can't say."

LAN CAO
An excerpt from Monkey Bridge[1]

Mai doesn't believe in the magic that's locked in my ears. She doesn't know that the story of my ears is the same as the story of my mother's life in the rice-growing province of Ba Xuyen. . . .My mother was not like other girls in Ba Xuyen. Born in the scalding heat of the equator, she had, after all, been named [Tuyet] after snow. And so she was by nature rebellious. And I became the perfect expression of her rebellion.

The moment I was born, I was already blessed with long, Buddha-shaped ears, so long that the rest of my face had to grow into them. "Push, push," my mother's midwife had yelled, her hands reaching inside to pull, pull, pull me by the head into the world. But as the midwife later told me, it was my ears, my long, long ears, that the midwife had touched, and it was by the ears that I was first tugged from my mother's womb. It was also with my magical ears that I could immediately hear gasps and sighs of the started neighbors who had gathered to watch the event of my birth. My ears, everyone must have noticed, were almost two times as big as my little newborn face. How many other people in this world can remember the sounds of their birth?

My ears, according to my mother, were ears reborn and made permanently whole to compensate for the stumps of pig ears that had been inflicted generationally on the girls of our village. Inside my ears were the rage and revenge of every girl from every generation before whose return with a shameful and earless pig had destroyed her family's lives . . . . Through my ears, my mother proclaimed, I would have the power not only to heal my mother's fear but also to repair generation after generation of past wrongs by healing the faces of karma itself.

*Michael L. Gray, "Selling Coke," photograph

PAULINE NEWTON

"Different Cultural Lenses": An Interview with Lan Cao[2]

October 24, 2000

Lan Cao, who remembers the Tết Offensive in Saigon, came to the United States from Vietnam in the 1970s. Her novel, Monkey Bridge, *as Cao explains in the following interview, emerged from a "few kernels of things that happened" during her early years in Vietnam and in the United States. Cao's work empowers its readers to visualize the bridges that a young immigrant must encounter and cross.*

Pauline Newton: In the opening pages of *Monkey Bridge*, your fiction debut, the reader is thrust by your main character, Mai, from a serene American hospital into the Vietnam/American war:

> Arlington Hospital was not a Saigon military hospital. . . .
> The American flag . . . still swelled and snapped in the
> wind. I knew I was not in Saigon. . . It was not 1968 but
> 1978. Yet I also knew, as I passed a wall of smoked-glass
> windows, that I would see the quick movement of green
> camouflage fatigues, and I knew. I knew the medic insignia
> on his uniform and I knew, I knew, what I would see next.
> His face, not the face before the explosion, but the face
> after, motionless in a liquefied red that poured from a
> tangle of delicate veins. (1-2)

With these flashback-riddled scenes, you weave a wonderful variety of threads. There's a thread on the Vietnam/American war, there's a thread on Vietnamese family traditions and there's a thread on American immigration experiences, and all these threads are woven together to demonstrate your characters' experiences in Vietnam and in the United States. In an interview with Susan Geller Ettenheim of *BookGrrl*, you said that *Monkey Bridge* is not "historical fiction" although it is classified as fiction and it recounts some actual events, to some degree, in your life. Would you call it creative nonfiction?[3]

Lan Cao: No, I would just call it fiction. . . . The focus is really on the story of a family, and that family lives in a period during the war in Vietnam and then the period after the war in Vietnam. I would not put the setting as the main character. Whereas with historical fiction, I would think of the historical event as equally the main character as the characters themselves, and this book is not at all nonfiction, nor is it historical fiction. I would just call it fiction with some historical details.

N: I wondered how autobiographical the story is. You say that it's not based on just the history of what was happening with the character during her lifetime. But how autobiographical are Mai and her mother in the story in relation to yourself and your actual life?

C: Well, the feelings, the emotions, perhaps, are autobiographical in that sense, but it is not a memoir, so it is not as if every event actually happened. A lot of it is reinterpreted, remade truth. So, parts of it are things I pick off from my own life, but that is why I did not want it in a memoir format. I did not want to be constrained by the truth of my own life. I only wanted to explore a few kernels of things that happened in my own life and go on from there and sort of reweave something different. So, it is not at all autobiographical in the sense of tit for tat.

N: I have seen other writers of nonfiction and fiction struggle to "think back through their mothers"—to quote Virginia Woolf—to a time which often takes place before their daughters' lifetime so sometimes they are thinking back on their mothers' lifetime before the daughters were alive. For example, in one scene in *Monkey Bridge*, Mai and the reader are plunged into a Vietnamese story that links maternal generations. In this passage [see page 102] Mai is the daughter. The narrator is Mai's mother, speaking of her mother, Mai's (supposed) grandmother. Do you find the process of interweaving narrative voices a difficult one?

C: Well it is natural, in fact, for me. When I write, my natural inclination is to shift between past and present. It's not an effort for me. It's not a design or a device. It just happens very naturally, shifting from past or present, because I think as an immigrant what happens is that when you look at an event or an object even in the present world, very often you view it the way you view it now as well as the way you view it in a different cultural context. So, because I have that baggage with me, I see an event and see it through two different cultural lenses almost simultaneously without even necessarily noticing it. It's now just a natural part of how I view things. So, the past/present is simultaneous to me and, therefore, also when I shift in the narrative, one event —

N: Shift to what?

C: Shift in narrative from mother to daughter. For example, it follows from the shift from past to present. So it's just natural for me, and sometimes I have to restrain myself from doing it too much because sometimes I know that readers want to get one story forward and finished rather than be interrupted. But past/present is just so — past/present, simultaneous voices. That's how I naturally think and naturally write, and if I do not do it that way it is my conscious design. So, it is the reverse, I think, of maybe the way other people write.[4]

N: In that same scene that I mentioned above, Mai is swept into her mother's world because she's found some notes handwritten in Vietnamese. Did your mother leave behind some actual letters for you that you used in conjunction with *Monkey Bridge*?

C: No, no, not at all. A totally made-up device. I cannot recall why it came out that way. It just did and I went with it.

N: That is interesting. Many of the female immigrants in my dissertation study came from Caribbean or South China Sea islands or peninsulas: Antigua, Puerto Rico, the Dominican Republic, Malaysia, and Vietnam. They often experience "islandness," which could be considered an insulated tropical lifestyle or isolation among other things, even after they migrate and adapt to the United States. Do you see an "islandness" in relation to your own life? And are there particular times in your life that you feel this "islandness" more acutely?

C: I think "islandness" would just be kind of a separation, I would say, right, in any moment of separation that one feels a gulf, between one's self and the outer world. Yes, it is just an issue of feeling separate from the outside world. I think anybody can feel "islandness." And, so in that way it is a very universal experience. Certainly, I can imagine that if one is an immigrant, let's say, coming to a new place, one would, as many recent immigrants do, remain within one's own enclave. One would have a separate community that is built and that community could be very self-sufficient, like, for example, a Chinatown. It has its own shops, supermarket, everything. It could be very self-sufficient and you could live there without ever venturing forth into the mainstream world. So, that is, immigrant communities can be islands in and of themselves. And, certainly, that would make one feel both a sense of community with one's own fellow immigrants, but it also would make one feel separate from the rest of the mainstream society. So I think that is a condition that many immigrants face, this feeling of isolation and community simultaneously because the community is separate from the outside world. At the same time, however, I do *not* think that that sense of "islandness" or isolation is really limited to any one group. One could be completely a part of the mainstream, the majority, and would still feel a psychic or a psychological "islandness." I think loneliness is a very common and universal human experience. It may have particular characteristics that are culture-related and that are related to one's personal experience of migration, but that is a particular variation of "islandness" and not the sole possession or the sole condition of being an immigrant. So I think in that way, many other people can relate to that feeling if that is what you write about.

N: What about your life particularly?

C: Well, the isolation was more intense at the beginning because I was still trying to cope, and as one moves forth and knows English and knows the ways of the new world, one feels less of that. But, again, as I say, that is an exterior form of "islandness." Now you have the tools to cope but I do not think that is the interior "islandness." I think people always feel lonely to a certain extent.

N: Shirley Geok-lin Lim, a Malaysian American, author of *Among the White Moon Faces*, states that writing her autobiography "forced [her] to deal with [her]self as an American."[5] Now that you have written about your experiences in American culture, how did writing enable you to find your own niche or island, if you will, in an American or in Vietnamese society?

C: I dealt with this before I wrote the book, so the book really did not help me come to terms with it one way or another. That sense of coming to terms — Is one an American? Is one a hyphenated American? There is now a new term, ampersand, which is Vietnamese&American rather than Vietnamese-American. There are all these different emphases. Do you focus on the ampersand? Do you focus on the hyphen? How do you define yourself? I think I grappled with those questions way before I wrote the book. So, the writing of the book sort of made the process more pronounced because one is now having to put it down on paper and express a feeling with your language. Any time you express your feeling in language, you change that feeling a little bit, just as in many ways writing a diary makes you think of an experience differently. Because sometimes when you write a diary or when you recount a story, it may make you feel about the story differently. But I did the process of grappling before I wrote the book. And, as far as finding niches is concerned, I have to tell you maybe it is really my own personality, because I think each of us copes and navigates our own life in different ways.

I was never interested in finding niches. I was always much more interested in bridges. And, I do believe in communities, say, for example, Orange County in California has a lot of Vietnamese — it is the largest Vietnamese American community in the U.S. — and I visited it when I was on sabbatical in California. I was really impressed by it and I thought it formed a wonderful function. And it is right for a lot of people to have that. Little Italys, Chinatowns, the Lower East Side for the early Jewish immigrants — those are all very important gathering places. It does not take away from the intrinsic value that those places have always had politically, economically, socially, psychologically for new immigrants that I tend to be more interested in staying within myself and making connections no matter where I am. But, for me, I would not want to live in those places, because it just does not fit in my own life. I have never sought out niches. I have always sort of found my own niche no matter where I am. Because I really think the niche is much more interior for me than geographically bound. I have cousins who came when they were even younger than I was who have remained very embedded in the Vietnamese community in Northern Virginia. They have never left it. They have married from within. They stay there. They are very interconnected. And I do not feel that I necessarily get automatic connections from people with whom I have cultural connections. I do not sense that. Sometimes it is more on an individual and personal basis for me. I do not think that a person from my own culture with my same history and my same growing-up experiences necessarily understands me more. Or that I can relate to that person more than a person who has nothing of that in common with me.

And that is why I like writing, because I think in literature, in fiction, you create your own world, and it's that own world when I meet a new person—if that person creates their own world also in a way that is compatible with mine—that is where I find the psychic connection. The creation of one's own identity, one's own world, one's own definition. Of course, with what we carry with us.

Nobody is an unencumbered person. We all come with our own inherited identity. . . . We all carry our own history with us that we inherit from our culture, our history, our ethnicity, and all of that. But I relate more to those who take that and make something else with it. It is that new world that is created from the old and the new. Those people who do that with me are the ones that I am more compatible with.

N: Mai, your character, tackles immigrant experiences such as a college interview at an American college "drunken-monkey style," or by means of the Vietnamese "art of evasion and distraction [and] not brute force" (129). What barriers or borders did you as an immigrant have to navigate or overcome in order to share your story?

C: Language. I think that probably the primary objective for me from '75 until '79 was learning English and overcoming the language barrier. Because you really need language to express yourself, obviously, in any world, and unless you can express yourself in a way that others can understand you, I think that your access to the predominant outside world will be very restricted. So, the moment the language issue was settled for me, that really was the main thing.

N: You were talking about finding people who have stepped out—who have bridged cultures. You relate to those people and I was wondering if your writing has been a means for you to find a community or some kind of family you share some of your concerns and interests with.

C: Yes. My friends, the people I feel close to, they are not necessarily all writers. But some are, and the others, even if they are not writers, they definitely are very interested in language and storytelling and reexamining the past. The problem I have found with those who are embedded in culture and history and community is a tendency in many ways to kind of allow the past to define them too much. The past—traditional communities—has a lot of prejudices, too. They are not necessarily models of openness nor are they necessarily models of understanding. They have a pretty oppressive side to them. They make you fit in. If you do not fit in you are ostracized. So community is great, but there are negative sides to community, and if you are forever community-defined, I find it to be intolerable, and so I like the idea of creating one's own community using the community one inherits but making it fit oneself in a way that is more conducive to individual growth.

N: Susan Sachs, author of "For Immigrants, a New American Dream," suggests that even though non-Anglo female immigrants constantly struggle to transcend their root cultures (in this case, your Vietnamese one) in order to become Americans, they never assimilate completely, unlike their Anglo-European "real and literary forebears."[6] Instead, these recent immigrants literally and figuratively become cross-cultural women of sundry lands and cultures. Does your immigrant status complicate or prohibit your "complete assimilation"?

C: Well, the process of going from immigration to Americanization is the process that really is the definition of this country and in this country, except for the African Americans who were not immigrants or the Native Americans who are also not immigrants; so excepting those two major groups in this country, this is a country of immigrants. It is defined by immigrants in a way that is very different, I would say, than another country that has a lot of immigrants. I guess what I am trying to say is France has a lot of immigrants. Germany has a lot of immigrants but I do not consider them to be a country of immigrants. It may very well be that Germany takes in more immigrants now than the U.S. I have no idea. But let's say it does not. In my mind, Germany will never be a country of immigrants the same way this country is a country of immigrants. This country is defined inextricably with its history of immigration. So, the idea of Americanization from the initial process of immigration is the idea of this country itself.

So in that way, any story that tells the story of immigration and Americanization would relate and have some kind of resounding effect to many Americans because a lot of people can trace their roots back to immigration of one form or another and every generation has faced this issue which is the issue of — How much do you retain of your own culture? How much do you shed your own culture? —and in the process you could very well end up psychologically murdering yourself in order to become somebody else. Right? And the process can be an extremely violent one. You can inflict great damage to yourself in order to make yourself into an image that is externally defined by whatever the Americanization, whatever an American is. You could very well do damage to yourself in the process. So, yes, these are, I think, things that every immigrant generation in the U.S. has faced and I do not think it is necessarily particular to Vietnamese immigrants.

But I do think that when you are non-Anglo, of a different race, then there is an additional complication. But that complication is not because of immigration. It is because of the race experience in this country. The immigration experience, I think, would be quite the same in terms of shedding or keeping your culture, the generational conflict between the new generation and the old generation, new food versus old food, McDonald's versus spaghetti. Whatever it is, it will always have that kind of thing. The race issue is a separate and totally different issue. Of course, there is no way that you are going to change your race and that will be something that you will always take with you, no matter how many generations you have been here.

That is an issue that I think is particularly unique to Asian immigrants primarily because, for some reason, Asian immigrants and Asian Americans tend not to be very concerned about public and political and social modes of assimilation. In other words, you do not see many Asian Americans on television. The representation of Asian Americans in public spheres is not particularly dominant or highlighted, and so basically, if they are at all, they always have an accent. So, in American eyes and the way popular culture has represented Asian Americans, they are always somehow retaining their foreignness. And the Chinese have been here since the 1800s, probably as long as many Italians, as long as many Irish, but I'll bet you every Chinese American whom you have met will have been asked, "Where do you come from?" I think that is a common experience that almost every single Asian in this country has been asked. They could have been born in this country. Their grandfather or grandmother could have been born in this country. It does not matter.

So I think that issue is an issue unique to Asians because that alienness will always remain with them. Whereas, for example, black Americans, African Americans, have a different history. They will not be asked where they come from. They will be asked other questions maybe equally problematic and equally difficult. But that is because there is a different history behind it. I do not think that this particular issue is a minor one. I think if you are constantly being reminded or being seen as the outsider, it makes it easier, for example, to allow Japanese Americans to be relocated to camps during World War II, because if you are seen as an alien, then you are in danger. I have no idea whether Doctor Lee, the fellow, the scientist in the lab in Los Alamos, is or is not a spy. But, if it is the case that he was singled out and nobody else was, then I find that problematic and the idea is, again, if he is of a certain race and he is more suspect, he is more alien; others are seen as more American. The idea that there are some groups that are more American than others, that is the problematic one to me. But that has to do with race and Asianness, in particular, and not immigration.

N: I find your references to the Bionic Woman in *Monkey Bridge* interesting because the Bionic Woman is kind of a mixture of parts, or as you say, "a little bit of Shaolin kung fu mixed with American hardware and American know-how" (9). Since you represent two or more cultures—as a Vietnamese American—do you see the Bionic Woman as a sort of alter ego to Mai or to yourself?

C: I love the Bionic Woman. I really, really, really liked it when I got here, because when I grew up, one of the things that was very popular in Vietnam was these kinds of martial arts novels. Every kid reads them and they are a series. Each story has about 10 volumes and so sometimes you rent the book and then you hurry up and you rent the next one. They are very addictive. And they always involve male heroes who are very good in martial arts but female heroes who are also very good in martial arts. In other words, it is interesting when you see stories, traditional stories that 7-, 8-, 9-, and 10-year-old children in Vietnam read. In other words, we do not have traditional stories of "Snow White" or "Sleeping Beauty" where Snow White has an evil stepmother and is promoting a kind of envy and competition among girls and women for this Prince Charming who is going to come. The Vietnamese kids read these stories where the male character, the main character, is extremely handsome, highly skilled in swordsmanship, but the main female character is always as equal or better and always self-sufficient and knows how to do martial arts just as well as her male counterpart. And in fact, many of the martial arts styles were invented by women historically, so in that sense, the idea of the female being able to defend herself is very traditional in the culture in which I was raised.

Then I came here and I saw the Bionic Woman. I really just saw the Bionic Woman as an American reincarnation of one of the female characters in one of these books. And so in many ways, the show functioned in helping me to learn English, because I loved watching it and listening to English—characters in the show speak English—but it also allows me a kind of harking back, a nostalgic sense. So, this is almost not just nostalgia, but also a visual representation of some of the books I read.

N: How has your Vietnamese culture's attitude toward women who express themselves vocally or in writing influenced your own voice?

C: The Vietnamese culture is in many ways traditional, but it is not traditional regarding women the way that people in the West may think of it. As I said, Vietnamese women have always been represented in a very independent way. They are not seen as needing male rescue. That is not part of the culture. They may be restrained in other ways, but the idea of one's identity deriving completely from the husband or the father, I do not see it. For example, we do not have foot-binding like the Chinese—the idea

that the woman must be foot bound in order to enhance her
dependence on the male or that she would have to be of a certain
class to hire people to carry her around. That is not in the history
of the country. There have always been women warriors in Vietnamese history so the idea of female weakness is not there.

N: A strong female working alongside a man then. Does the
Vietnamese land itself influence roles of men and women because
of the rural way of life?

C: Yes, farming is very labor-intensive, especially rice planting.
And so both men and women are needed to do both. Men do the
plowing and women do the transplanting of the rice, which is a
very arduous and time-consuming process. Therefore, maybe just
from an economic perspective alone, the society could not have
afforded to bind the feet of women because they need women's
labor. You can certainly look at that from an economic perspective.
So, I never grew up with the sense of women being depicted as
needing male protection. Vietnamese culture, however, does place
a premium on female sacrifice[7] and often sacrifice for the husband.
That is seen very much as a virtue. If a woman made sacrifices in
order to do things for herself, that could be seen as selfish. But the
epitome of female virtue would be a woman who, even though she
is very strong and could be alone and does not need male protection, nonetheless decides to sacrifice herself completely for her
husband and the children.
    The idea of female sacrifice is the paragon of female virtue.
So it has its own version of what the appropriate female behavior
would be. I think that it is important, though, that I never did
grow up with a sense of the woman being somehow weak. And
you would not see a Vietnamese movie where the heroine is—you
see this all of the time in Hollywood movies—the female is running. The male is the stereotype of somebody bad pursuing the
female and at the last minute—she is wearing high heels so—she
always falls. It is like the standard thing—she always falls and
then gets caught and then saved by a man. That just would not be
in the Vietnamese psyche to make that kind of ridiculous theme.
Because she would have taken her shoes off. She would not be
wearing high heels and running. She just would not be. It is a
male fantasy of a particular culture to make that type of a movie
and I do not think that the male, the Vietnamese male, fantasy

would be seeing a woman vulnerable and falling. He may have his own fantasy. I am not saying that the Vietnamese male may not have his own very particular gendered fantasy but it would not be expressed that way.

N: You end *Monkey Bridge* with Mai's entrance into Mount Holyoke. She is still young. She still faces that inevitable "one wrong move, one moment off guard" in which she might, say, watch her friend play a chord on a piano in an American music store and suddenly see her friend's trigger finger transform into a war-image of "a blanched, pulpy stump of gauze and bandages that moved spastically like the severed remnant of a lizard's tail" (28).[8] She has not undergone the transition of going to college or taken a lover. Why did you choose to end the book without exploring her continuing development?

C: Because I only wanted to see the initial stage in which she made the decision to leave the Vietnamese community and I wanted to show her at the door as she is exiting, and it really almost does not matter what she ultimately decides after that. What is important is that she took the first step.

---

1. Lan Cao, *Monkey Bridge* (New York: Penguin Books, 1997), 46-47; 51-52. Cao's italics. Subsequent citations appear parenthetically in the text.

2. Special thanks to Lillian Potter and Lisa Wellinghoff for their assistance with transcription.

3. Lan Cao, "Crossing Bridges: Bookgrrl Interviews Lan Cao," interview by Susan Geller Ettenheim, in *Bookgrrl 7* June 2000 <http://www.cybergrrl.com/fun/bookgrrl/art373>.

4. Cao may shift between narrative techniques effortlessly, but for Le Ly Hayslip, author of *When Heaven and Earth Changed Places* and *Child of War, Woman of Peace*, the narrative writing process is a laborious, conscious one, due in part to her limited formal education, though she is driven to write. She desires to "give a voice [to] the Vietnamese villagers": "I want to help the Americans and the people around the world to understand what the [Vietnam/American] war did to innocent people like myself and my family and other villagers. And the more I read other books, the more I want these people to have a voice. . . . And that is the point . . . . It's not

my voice, but a vehicle between spirits and people" (Le Ly Hayslip, "Bringing Together the United States and Vietnam: An Interview with Le Ly Hayslip," interview by Pauline T. Newton, tape recording, 20 November 2000 in "Transcultural Women of Late Twentieth-Century U.S. American Literature: First-Generation Immigrants from Islands and Peninsulas," by Pauline T. Newton [Ph.D. dissertation, The University of Tulsa, 2002], 247-248).

5. Shirley Geok-lin Lim, "Interview with Shirley Geok-lin Lim: Writing a Sense of Self," interview by Sook C. Kong, 22 November 1997, 9 September 2000 <http://www.alba.org/xfrontpage/lim.htm>.

6. Susan Sachs, "For Immigrants, a New American Dream," *The New York Times* 9 January 2000, NE 21, NE 23.

7. Hayslip, too, emphasizes Vietnamese "female sacrifice": "the Vietnamese woman is much more responsible in a family household. . . .Women had to do all the other things at home like please her parents on both her husband's side and her own side. Take care of her children. Make sure they had food to eat and were educated. Make sure her husband was safe in a battle zone. Make sure ancestors were worshipped. Make sure of interaction within the community. And, all at the same time, you see, fight in the war. Vietnam is as it is today, because of the women, the culture. The tradition has been intact for so many years because of women. Not men. Because men destroy everything. Women are the ones who hold everything together. And so the Vietnamese woman's role is much deeper . . . . We always sacrifice" (Hayslip 251-252).

8. Cao clarifies later in this passage the reason for the vivid image of a cut-off finger: the Vietnamese often cut "off the index fingers of boys to avoid the draft . . ." (Cao 28).

ANH CHI PHAM

A Day At Home

In the morning, I pour myself a cup of grandfather's tea. It's so strong, I gag at the bitterness. Out of curiosity, I lift the clay lid and see inside a mass of tangled black leaves. I scavenge through the fridge, stocked with giant bags of bok choy, my brother's leftover KFC lunch, my parents' vegetarian meats, and tubs of soups and noodles. There's tofu pudding, which I drown in honey-colored sugar water and nuke for a few minutes.

I take the steaming bowl outside to the patio where grandfather is stringing tinsel over the koi pond. He says that cranes have gotten to the fish again. I'm surprised there are any cranes in Southern California; it seems so dry and barren here. The tinsel, held up by juniper shrubs and lemon trees, looks like a mad Christmas decoration; its criss-crossing lines shine gaudily above the water.

After breakfast, I shower and read in my old room. Van has turned it into a child's room full of stuffed animals, Hello Kitty paraphernalia, pictures encased in heart-shaped frames, and letters from her friends in Vietnam. She's nineteen, the same age I was when I left home.

Later in the day, I watch a documentary about the Flying Wallendas, a circus family known for crossing tightropes in a seven-person pyramid; four on the rope, two in the middle, and one person on top, sitting on a chair. In 1952, the famous seven fell. There is a picture of the accident; the white chair hanging in mid-air, the bodies askew, falling every which way, but suspended forever in the falling. That day, two Wallendas died, and the youngest was crippled, but the patriarch, compelled by anger and grief, an insolent desire to defy fate, willed his family to do the stunt again. There's no footage of the crossing, but I imagine them, each fighting off memory, each walking the tightrope, step by step in careful concentration, and every once in a while someone adjusting ever so slightly to keep balance with the others. Like this they must have crossed to the other side, one by one, exhaling the moment a foot touches the platform, one by one, until all seven stand victorious.

My grandfather walks by, smoking his pipe, as the aged patriarch, now many years later, falls ten stories to his death. He asks me what happened, thinking that it is the news and I tell him in broken Vietnamese that it's a documentary about a circus family who walks over ropes. They're famous for their seven-person pyramid. I want to tell him about the accident, about the resurrection, but the patriarch's body is lying on the ground, and I cannot find the words as my grandfather walks away.

During dinner, Van and my brother joke about her being a communist. They trade barbs and plates of food across the table. I don't understand most of the jokes, but I can feel the lightness. I wonder if my parents ever thought that there would be a day like this, when they would be hosting their brother's daughter, when they would think that the differences between them were funny.

After dinner, my father turns on the Lakers game while my brother washes the dishes, and Van and I clean. Grandmother is in her room watching dubbed Hong Kong movies. From the bathroom, I hear water running; my mother must be washing her hair. After twenty-one years, she still refuses to shower in the morning and I know that after twenty more, it would still be foreign to her. Outside, my grandfather smokes from his pipe, his silhouette dark against the salmon-colored sky.

As I wipe the table, he slides the screen door open and whispers to me: come here, come here. I walk over to the sliding door and see a white crane standing on the tool shed. He must be three or four feet tall, but on top of the tool shed, he towers over us. His white body glows in the evening light. One by one, my family comes to the door to look at the crane, my father holding his wine glass, Van with her bright eyes, my brother talking loudly until we motion for him to stop, my mother, wet hair dripping, and my grandmother already in her pajamas. Huddled together like this, the seven of us marvel at the ghostly figure. The crane stands still and godlike, a pearl at dusk.

MICHAEL L. GRAY
The Tiger Cup

An accident seemed inevitable, I only wondered if someone would be killed. One after another, a stream of small motorbikes screamed along the road, within a few feet of thousands of enthralled spectators, cheering the racers on. It was September 1998 and Vietnam had just beaten Thailand in the semi-finals of the Tiger Cup soccer championship. A highway on the outskirts of Hanoi had become an impromptu racetrack in celebration of the victory. Although this type of illegal motorbike racing was not new in Vietnam, a winning soccer team was unheard of. The two were nonetheless connected, as it was soccer that brought people onto the streets—and onto their motorbikes.

The Tiger Cup pits the top eight Southeast Asian national teams against one another. Held every two years, it does not rank very high among international festivals of sport. But its importance in Southeast Asia is unrivalled. This was the first time the event was held in Vietnam. Thailand was favored coming into the tournament, but Vietnam had home-field advantage. The Thai team had been shaken by scandal in their last game—a 3-2 farce of a win over Indonesia. (The Indonesians had scored on themselves, intentionally, to avoid a semi-final match-up against Vietnam in Hanoi). Vietnam played with passion, and a little luck, and triumphed 3-0.

This was during my second year in Vietnam, after I returned from graduate studies in London. As during my first year in Hanoi, in 1995, I was working at the *Vietnam News*, which, to put it mildly, I did not find very stimulating. I figured the Tiger Cup would provide a good chance to do some more interesting writing. The *Vietnam News* office was a little chaotic at the best of times, and after a national triumph like beating Thailand, no one wanted to work. We did, however, have a paper to put out the next day. Sensing we would need a photo of the inevitable celebration—the

*Michael L. Gray, photograph

photographer was stuck at the stadium—I grabbed my camera and headed out onto the streets, about twenty minutes after the game ended. The stadium is several kilometers away from downtown, but within minutes of the victory a mass of motorbikes careened down Hai Ba Trung Street in central Hanoi. Each carried two, sometimes three or four, jubilant fans waving red flags through the air and shouting *"Vietnam, vo địch!"* (Vietnam, champions!). Adorned in red clothes and face paint, people of all ages were overjoyed to win in the semi-finals—the first time soccer-mad Vietnam could claim to be the favorites in any league or tournament.

The crowd carried me along for a few blocks, until at the corner of Hai Ba Trung and Ba Trieu streets, just south of Hoan Kiem Lake in the heart of the downtown, I climbed a street pole already covered with kids, to get some shots from above the masses. After continuing up to the lake, I turned back towards the office, as I still had some headlines to write for tomorrow's issue.

The sports editor, Steve, was busy writing up the match report, and wanted to know if I had any pictures. It was now almost 11:00 p.m. and our photographer had given up on having photos developed. But I had spotted one lab on Ba Trieu Street that was still open. We called to confirm and then I headed back to the crazy corner of Ba Trieu and Hai Ba Trung. This time I locked my bike on the sidewalk and strode out to the middle of the road, bikes whizzing past from all directions. I finished off the roll, dropped it off at the lab—now full of press photographers—and again headed back to the office. Only Steve was still working, as everyone else had gathered around a large bottle of gin, unopened as yet. I was sweating from the heat and the action, but I knew the night was just beginning. As the evening progressed the atmosphere outside would change. When the crowds thinned, young men would pick up the speed of their bikes, and the racing would be on.

Like most Westerners arriving in Hanoi, the first thing I noticed was the traffic. It was everywhere at once, and the only order seemed to be a passive chaos where people relied on the random probability of survival to determine their trajectory, rather than looking both ways, for example, or following an established body of traffic laws. This first impression soon looked somewhat unfair; within days of arriving I was on a bicycle myself and "part of the problem," as the truly innocent might put it. I did not have any serious accidents my first year in Vietnam, when there were only a few traffic lights in all of Hanoi, and people coasted through intersections without looking or slowing their pace, let alone stopping. For one month I rode a bike that had no brakes, so I can hardly complain about other people. Furthermore, I cherish the sights I saw on the roads of Hanoi every day. A frail old man in tweed coat and French beret, swamped by midday traffic on his olive green Babetto. Or two dead pigs being shipped across town in a cyclo, blood dripping from their nostrils as their fat white legs jiggled up and down from the bumpy ride. I once saw seven human beings on a small 50cc scooter—two adults and five children. Three adults is standard; four, occasional.

But despite this romantic vision of the quaint madness of it all, the reality is that many people die horrible deaths on the road in Vietnam. Traffic accidents and congestion are the most serious social problems in urban areas, apart from land conflicts for housing space. The Hanoi municipal government's efforts to solve traffic problems have not always been effective. Enormous roads have been built that lead nowhere, and the police do not exactly have a good reputation for community service. Unfortunately, people will continue to die, and there is very little that can be done about it. If the experience of Western countries is anything to judge by, attitudes towards safety change very slowly. Of more importance to me here, however, is the culture surrounding the "motorcycle cult" in modern Vietnam. The motorbike that a person chooses to sit on is quickly becoming a reflection of individual character. It is the most visible and important element in the spread of the consumer culture in Vietnam.

People are piling onto a greater variety of increasingly colorful and expensive motorbikes. Remember that Vietnamese society has its roots in Confucian conformism. As in the West, where cars and motorbikes have long been seen as an expression of their owners' tastes, different makes and models are starting to carry social significance. Whereas in 1995 everyone aspired to own a **Honda Dream**, by 1998 people were buying bikes for the "look" they wanted to present. The Dream is the classic "family sedan" that very often carries dad, mom, grandma and two or three kids all on a three-foot long cushion. It is the conservative choice— available in any color you want, as long as it's brown. But while the Dream is the dependable and reliable option, it's not the cheapest—the Honda name always comes at a price and the Dream goes for about $2,400 new (Hanoi's per capita income is somewhere just under $1,000 year).

The **Honda Wave** is the choice for slightly hipper, younger people who still want the Honda name, but attached to something with brighter colors and a peppier 110cc engine. The Wave was Honda's answer to the **Suzuki Viva**, which in 1998 was the hottest thing on the road. Flashier than the Dream, the Viva came with a 110cc engine and most models had a front disk brake instead of a drum. Now the Viva is old news. It was supplanted by the Wave, which is so popular there are now several Chinese copies, including one that looks exactly like the real thing, except that it is labelled "Hongda Wife." The Chinese copies cost about $500, which makes them hard to resist despite their dubious quality.

An extremely expensive bike is the **Honda Spacy**, which has small, fat wheels like the classic Italian scooters. At over $4,500, the Spacy is a favorite of yuppies who want the super-comfortable, almost hands-free ride. In midtown traffic you can file your nails or gab on your cell phone, no problem.

The Honda I love is a Thai-built model called the **Weasel**. Another of my favorites is the **Babetto**, used by very old men and farmers. It's a tiny Italian scooter that looks like a bicycle, and even has pedals.

The main machine for hot young punks who want to race around town at breakneck speed is the **Suzuki FX125**, a two-stroke, 125cc, five-speed pocket-rocket. Young Vietnamese men who ride bikes like this weave from side to side, even when driving down a straight, empty road. Late-night racers rely on this model above all others to scare their own pants off. Another Suzuki is the **GN125**—the man's-man bike. Motorbikes in Vietnam are gendered, and registration cards for this bike say it is a "male" motorcycle. This is because it actually has a clutch, and looks almost like a real motorbike. Still, it's only 125cc. Others in this category include a range of bikes made to look exactly like Harley Davidsons, except when you get close you realize they still only have 125 or 150cc engines. These are the "tough-guy bikes" favored by cops and other gangsters.

The **Minsk** is a Russian bike, very popular with young expatriates. It is extremely loud and unreliable, but although small (125cc) it at least *feels* like a real motorbike. Vietnamese do not drive this bike, except farmers. They also do not seem to understand why foreigners love it so much. There is a "Minsk Club" in Hanoi run by a group of young expats who do a lot of riding up in the mountains. So it's the cult favorite.

Another expensive bike popular with yuppies is the **Piaggio Vespa**. Piaggio also has a number of smaller, brightly colored models that are very popular with young women. They're like the Honda Spacy, but more fun to color-coordinate with your shoes. Finally, there is the **Yamaha Majestic**. This thing looks like a spaceship, and is clearly intended to blow the Spacy off the road. Incredibly expensive and quite large, it is perhaps the ultimate ride for the nouveaux riche — at least those who can't afford cars.

Motorbike racing began soon after *doi moi,* or "renovation" took effect in the late 1980s. *Doi moi* was a series of reforms, similar to those in China, which freed up the economy from tight state control. Young Vietnamese in the 1990s found an independence they had never known. This was most apparent when parents handed over the keys to the family motorbike. Young men began racing their bikes around the city at night in what quickly became an underground cult. Some events were organized, and races from Hanoi to Hai Phong were said to offer a Honda Dream to the winner. Some of the racers would cut their brake cables and wrap white bandanas around their heads (a death symbol). People would line the streets on weekend nights to watch them scream past.

The government went on the offensive with a barrage of propaganda campaigns against "social evils," but youths were not responding. Many of the worst offenders, as it turned out, were the sons of high-ranking officials. Eventually, the police cracked down on racing in the downtown area, particularly as a common route passed by the Ho Chi Minh Mausoleum at Ba Dinh Square. Barricades were put up on some streets, and water trucks sprayed the streets to deter speeding. But there were too many streets, too many bikes, and clearly, too many disaffected youth.

This new-found freedom animated the streets the night Vietnam beat Thailand in the Tiger Cup. The pictures were done by 11:45 p.m., so once again I ventured into the mayhem, shooting more photos on the way to the lab. The streets had not calmed at all and the adrenaline was flowing as I sped along at a brisk pace. By the time I returned to the office, the gin was open and everyone was toasting Vietnam's success. The pictures were not brilliant, but we found one that looked okay. Leaving the sports editor to his work, I retired to a nearby bar where my friends were waiting. Now, well after midnight, I sat down to a pint of beer. We stayed at the bar until almost 2:00 a.m. There were four of us: myself along with Eric, another Michael—a reporter for a wire agency —and his young interpreter, Giang. Leaving the bar we immediately found ourselves on a packed boulevard. Vehicles of all kinds draped with people and red flags formed an animated chain several kilometers long. One could only go with the flow. Groups of bikes a thousand-strong formed huge snakes that would occasionally cross—and collide—at intersections, slowing the pace but not the buzz of revelry. The trail of bikes eventually led to the highway running along the east edge of Hanoi, near the Red River. Most of the riders were heading across the main bridge to Gia Lam district, a very poor suburb of little repute outside the numerous brothels that lined either side of the main road. Michael and Eric did not seem thrilled about venturing into Gia Lam. "Let's not get mugged tonight," Eric mumbled. But I knew Gia Lam was one of the only places where there would be bike races. The police presence in the center of Hanoi was too strong, even for those already deranged enough to wind up a 100cc scooter to speeds approaching 100km per hour on crowded streets. We made our way over the bridge, stopping halfway across to photo-graph a crowd of motorbikes racing back in the other direction.

In Gia Lam the road leading from the bridge was packed. By Vietnamese standards it was a freeway: four lanes separated by a small concrete divider painted red and white. From the top of the road, where it rises up to meet the bridge, one could see thousands of people lining either sidewalk. An almost equal number of riders weaved in and out of the regular traffic, which at that time of night was only cargo trucks bringing goods from Hai Phong port, as well as some hapless farmers trying to bring their produce into the city. We waited at the top of the road to see what was going on. The mood had somehow changed from a celebration of victory to something more expectant: A nervous energy filled the crowd, which was now mainly young men, although some women were watching or riding pillion on the bikes. The circuit started at the top of the road where the divider began. The riders continued down about two or three kilometers to an intersection where the divider broke off again. There they would round the corner and return to the top.

As we watched from the edge of the bridge, the speed of the bikes began to pick up. There were now few people waving flags and shouting about the game. Many of the motorbikes, especially the quick Suzuki Vivas, had their mufflers punctured or entirely cut off, so they howled like formula racing bikes. To get into the heart of the crowd we headed down the road, but bikes began roaring past us and for safety's sake we pulled to the side about one kilometer from the bridge. We stuck out because there were no other Westerners in sight, but the attention was soon back on the road. Eric stood on his parked bike to film the scene with his video camera, while the other Michael and I ventured a few feet onto the road with our cameras.

"It's not really a race," one of the spectators later said, "it's just a sport gathering."

With no finish line and no prize money involved, the riders were simply screaming around in a circle for show. The scene was like a European rally, with the crowd leaning out onto the raceway only to pull back as bikes whipped by. Through the lens of my camera I saw bikes carrying one, two, or even three people whipping past at outrageous speeds. It was not enough for the young men to ride quickly; they also jerked and weaved their bikes from side to side to get the full effect of the speed and impress the crowd. Some lowered their kickstands, to send up a shower of sparks whenever they leaned to the left. It was an awesome sight.

After snapping several photos, I panned back up the street to see one of the fastest bikes weave and clip the concrete divider. Before the rider could regain control he smashed into a second bike and they both flew through the air. The crowd gasped collectively, watching as the first rider jumped up onto the divider to avoid any more contact—while the second lay completely motionless on the road. A few more bikes tore past before someone from the crowd sprinted across the road to check the condition of the downed man. A panicked expression appeared on the spectator's face and he waved more people over. Soon the entire street was packed with people surrounding the fallen rider. They pulled him off the road while people surged forward to get a look.

"*Chet roi! chet roi!*" people yelled, which literally means "he's dead" but is a common expression whenever misfortune strikes. We pushed forward ourselves, Michael still snapping photos. In the pandemonium I couldn't see the rider, but the crowd was shifting and moving, which made me think the man was on his feet or moving himself. I eventually caught sight of someone with blood streaming from his head, but this could also have been the first rider. Whether serious injury had occurred or not, the crowd soon dispersed and the bikes were pulled off the road. With first blood spilled, the racing continued at an even faster pace.

Although this type of racing is not as common as it once was, the state media still mention it as one of the "evils" threatening social peace. Young men in many nations take part in dangerous sporting events that are more ritual than competition—the running of the bulls in Pamplona perhaps the most famous example. And unlike the rioting that sometimes accompanies European and American sports, there was no threat of violence anywhere to be seen. But as with rioting, part of the attraction for young hooligan-racers in Vietnam is the illegal nature of their actions. In a country where both political and social restrictions limit people's ability to express themselves, any occasion where there is mass celebration—with even the police letting down their guard—youths take the opportunity to test the bounds of permissible behavior. It all starts with soccer, which is by far the number one cause for mass celebration in Vietnam. Many nations around the world are soccer-mad, but I was still surprised at the degree to which Vietnamese people followed European soccer, from the other side of the world.

Events surrounding the 1998 World Cup demonstrated this sharply. In the months leading up to the Cup, Vietnam was wracked by a serious drought. In early May, the director of Electricity Vietnam imposed power cuts as water levels fell drastically in reservoirs around the country. Eighty percent of the country's power comes from hydro-electricity, and if no rain fell by mid-May, the turbines at Hoa Binh dam would be shut down. The dam supplies power to Hanoi and much of northern and central Vietnam. The electricity director asked people to switch off lamps and air conditioners, and municipal authorities across the country were told to suspend the use of all neon signs in advertising. Things were getting very grave for people all over the country. Crops were starting to wither, industrial output was being affected, and the World Cup was approaching. With no rain, the material life of the people was in immediate peril. But this year, blackouts would also mean no television, and no television would mean no World Cup.

Thousands of dollars in agricultural revenue were lost, and permanent damage to coffee trees was imminent. Rumors spread that the government was re-routing power to Hanoi and Saigon, at the expense of the provinces. People were becoming desperate. Tempers flared. Still, no rain. And the nation waited. The crops were a lost cause — but it was no longer rain that people were waiting for. They wanted an assurance, a guarantee, a strong voice to tell them everything would be all right. This came on June 9, when the public relations director of the Hanoi Power Company called a press conference to say that power cuts would not occur during the World Cup. Fresh rumors had it the government was worried about major social upheaval and instability if the Cup could not be viewed by all the masses. The Hanoi Power Company went so far as to say, "Football fans can count on power company technicians to be available if any electricity lines break down."

This had a calming effect, but it was soon the least of concerns for people in the capital city. June 10 arrived and the Cup started. Games were broadcast live in the middle of the night. The first match saw Scotland robbed of victory by shoddy refereeing. There were no power cuts and every single television set in the nation was tuned to the football. Cafés were open all hours, and at night a bright flickering light could be seen every twenty paces or so on otherwise empty streets. A small crowd would be gathered at each screen, still and silent until a goal and everyone screaming *VAO!!*

There had even been rain on the weekend. A lot of rain. The heavens opened and more rain hit the city in four days than was normal in a month. Downpours of over ten centimeters became a nightly event. Now people wanted the rain to go away. The modernization of Hanoi's drainage system had not kept pace with other infrastructure developments. The city was backed up like a crudely made toilet. Water up to a meter high swamped streets all over town. But in misery there is happiness. And in Hanoi, there was electricity and the World Cup. Television shop owners were making more money than ever, and many started renting out sets by the day. Breweries couldn't keep pace and the price of instant noodles and soft drinks went through the roof. Caffeine-rich coffee saw a 40 percent price hike. Some people had booked annual leave to correspond with the month of the Cup, while others caught a mysterious fever and called in sick. Television sets were provided for convicts, such was the spirit of brotherly love and celebration.

Some people were losing it. On June 23 a newspaper reported that one football fan electrocuted himself after biting through a live cable in an effort to restore the reception on his set.

A few days later, a man killed himself after losing his Honda Dream motorbike in World Cup betting. Even monks were getting in on the action. They had no money so they bet free breakfasts and dishwashing duty. Karaoke bar owners were cursing the Cup as business dropped off. Prostitutes publicly complained that their customers were either busy watching games or too tired to shag. Trade union delegates postponed their annual conference. Fights were noted and one person was stabbed after the Netherlands-Mexico match. All this and the second round had not even started. And this was nothing compared to the Tiger Cup.

The Southeast Asian tournament took place only a few months after the World Cup ended. After witnessing Hanoi in the middle of World Cup madness, I thought I was prepared for the Tiger Cup. But I was amazed at the level of danger involved in post-soccer racing. It is an understatement to say that older Vietnamese—witnesses to decades of war and poverty—would have been disturbed by the scene I saw unfold in Gia Lam. The first generation born after the war were putting life and limb at risk for no apparent reason, while looking on were thousands of hip city youths, dozens of prostitutes from the hotels lining the raceway, and a few absolutely stunned peasants still trying to get their veggies into the city. Then, at 3:30 a.m., with startling speed, the crowd dispersed. The blue flashing light of a police van could be seen a kilometer down the road. The van eventually went by, with only one confiscated motorbike in the back. No mass arrests took place, but clearly the threat was enough to send people home. The year before, there had been at least one skirmish with police, and heavy sentences were levied on several youths who had burned a police car and injured some cops.

We decided to interview a few people at the scene. Michael talked briefly with one of the prostitutes, while her gold chain-laden pimp tried to push her on me. Then Michael found a young, very beautiful woman who had been on the back of a bike that pulled over quickly when the cops arrived. She answered in curt, short sentences—but clearly liked the idea of being interviewed by a foreign reporter.

"Sometimes people get killed, but riders aren't afraid of dying," she said.

When asked if any of her friends had died, she said: "No, but I don't care. I would still race if one my friends was killed."

As the interview continued, the enchanted reporter's questions became less and less newsworthy.

"So, do you ever drive the bike instead of your boyfriend?" Michael asked.

"It's my bike," she replied. "I drive it if I want to."

Finally pulling our friend away from his interview, we got on our Hondas and headed for home—drag-racing briefly on the now empty road. Back in Hanoi there was still a crowd on the highway running along the river, but the energy had drained away and there was no high-speed racing. We continued in the direction of home, passing an enormous pack of kids on bicycles, pedaling around and banging on drums at 4:00 a.m. Too young and too slow to hang with the motorbikes, they were nonetheless having a party of their own.

A truck then went past us filled with helmeted, stun-gun-toting riot police. We turned and followed, but were surprised when they did nothing to disperse the crowd. Some young men were still weaving along the street at a fast pace, but the cops did nothing but throw an empty plastic water bottle at one bike as it flew by. The disappointing riot police soon retired to the top of Hoan Kiem Lake, where many of their comrades were gathered to reflect back on the night's events. We headed home as well. There was still Saturday's final against Singapore, after all. I thought of the young racer's last words as we left her:

"What will happen on Saturday after Vietnam plays?" Michael had asked.

"We'll race."

The Temple of the Jade Emperor, Ho Chi Minh City

Everyone goes to hell
who does not go to Nirvana,
the boy tells me, making himself
my guide at the Jade Emperor

Temple. In another courtyard,
another country, I was shooed away—
My God sees you. You have no God
that lives. My God means nothing

to you. But here, twenty small children fly
to me and into their greeting—
hel-lo, hel-lo—which they seem to ride
like a swing. Into my arms a woman

presses a toddler—*Bring her to your country. Take her.*
There is nothing for her here. Sparrows
and sunlight are everywhere. I unwrap the fingers
from my fingers and she takes my ankles.

Where, I wonder, would the vendors say are the souls
of the three men whose skulls they'd offered
me in the market—cut in two, hinged at the brows,
festooned with charms of brass and silver?

A girl presses a starling into my palm:
Release him for our New Year. Make a prayer.
It will come true. She presses harder
until I think the bird will splatter in my hand.

She wants a dollar. In a courtyard
off a courtyard are legions of beautiful
urns, a snapshot taped on each—children, mostly—
attentive as if waiting for the day they can walk

out of their photos. A side altar is piled with fruit
and flowers, spoiling beside a girl's picture.
She has the bangs of a student
with whom I once was half in love,

she seems about to blow them out of her eyes.
"A spirit loosed and wandering"
moves through my mind like a wind.
At dusk the temple fills with sparrows

flying among golden demons and gods:
God of Money, God of War, God of Orphans,
God of the Poor—from outside, children
keep calling, *Hel-lo, Hel-lo*.

James Tuong Nguyen, photograph

BARBARA CROOKER

The Mothers

I
We gathered to give a baby shower
in absentia, for the yet-to-be-born,
two-thousand-miles-away first grandson
of a friend whose youngest child died
binge drinking. Grief, the uninvited guest,
squeezed in, sat down on the sofa. But we oohed
and aahed at the tiny sweaters, booties, rattles, bonnets.
We know the end of the story,
but we love the beginning anyway.
We filled our china plates with shrimp,
broccoli quiche, cream puffs, lemon squares,
talked about our grown children,
and the one who wasn't there.

II
Later, at the art museum,
two Vietnamese children from the family
sponsored by our church were chosen
for the Emerging Masters' Recital,
Paul on cello, Angela on violin.
I sat next to my friend Kathy,
and we remembered our work —
me teaching English as a Second Language,
her negotiating Social Services — and how if we'd known
how hard it was going to be, we'd have never signed up.
But aren't we all refugees, searching for our lives,
and don't we all become orphans in the end?

III
And now I'm at the university, seeing
"The Vagina Monologues," where my red-
headed middle daughter is playing a black
homeless lesbian, and where I am so lost
in the power of the words, for a short while
I forget who she is, shining in her cherry taffeta
prom dress from Goodwill. At the end, the play shifts
from the sexual to the sacred, the opening between
two worlds, the way we all came in, part of the wheel,
the hoop, the great turning.

James Tuong Nguyen, photograph

MICHAEL McCOLLY

The Forever Life of the Dragon

Tuong finds me standing in the late morning sun in the parking lot of Tan Son Nhut Airport, runs up from behind and nearly tackles me. "You finally make it!" He looks the very part of the American "Vietkiew"—stylish shin-length jeans, Nike shirt and baseball cap, sunglasses, and flip-flops. He throws down his cigarette and takes my bag, then stops in the middle of the parking lot, "Wait! Let me take your picture. First picture, right?"

Indeed that was the plan we'd discussed back in Chicago. He would translate and photograph, as I explored his country to learn how Vietnam is trying to face a spreading epidemic of HIV that has been doubling every year since 1994.

I have come from Thailand and before that India on a journey of sorts to see for myself what this pandemic is and why it is moving with alarming speed through Asia. Doctors told me in India that the numbers infected were probably twice the governmental projection of 3.7 million. And things were worse, I was told, in Myanmar, Laos, and Cambodia. In China, after years of denial that it had more than a few cases of this "Western disease," the government finally admitted AIDS was a problem. In six weeks I quickly understood what many activists had been saying for the past couple of years, that if Asian countries don't do something now, the rates of infection would soar, dwarfing the disaster in sub-Saharan Africa.

I'd met Tuong in my second year of teaching at a small university in northwest Chicago that served an ever-growing community of immigrants from just about every corner of the earth. He would have come and gone too like the others if it hadn't been for the fact that he had such trouble with his essays that I had to ask him to retake the class. And so over a year I must have read certain essays so many times that I felt I'd written them myself. After that, I thought I was finished with him, but then he was outside my office asking me to take a look at an essay for another class. And then he would sit down and ask how I was and, before I knew it, I'd be going over his essay page after page. Sometimes, I must admit I'd look down the hall and see him hovering outside my office and turn around and go get a cup of coffee, hoping he'd be gone when I got back. But then one day he came by my office to show me some photographs he'd taken. He'd decided to major in photography, a bold choice for an Asian-American immigrant. And when he flipped open his portfolio, I was stunned: they were all close-ups of the weathered and wild faces of street people in Uptown, one of Chicago's poorest neighborhoods and the home of the Vietnamese community.

The streets of Ho Chi Minh City at midday are clogged with motorbikes. Businesses and street vendors buzz with activity. I have no idea where we are or where we are going. I'd lived in West Africa as a Peace Corps volunteer and thought I knew what heat was, but here in June the humidity penetrates the skin and makes you feel as if your flesh is evaporating. The city stretches out into farmlands overtaking rice paddies. Polluted pools of stagnant water run along crumbling roads. As peasants migrate into the city from the poorer regions of the north, Ho Chi Minh City swarms with now nearly 6 million people, doubling in size in only twelve years. We pass four- or five-story cement apartments with iron grating over windows and clothes hanging on hangers from lines not to dry but simply because there are no other place to hang them. There seems to be an order, a holding back of the masses of things and people. Children and young people dominate every vista; Vietnam is one of the world's most densely populated countries and nearly 60 percent of its people are under the age of 25.

I check myself, mile after mile, anxious and exhausted from being on the road alone for 3 months. I am glad to be in Vietnam with Tuong and his family, who have gathered together for the first time since they dispersed in the early 90s. Here, if I get sick, I know they will take care of me.

It was Tuong, after all, who had the guts to come into my office that day four years ago and ask what no faculty member seemed able to, though some were aware something was wrong. "You look so sad all the time. Are you okay?" The directness of his words and his open face felt like a push that knocked me backward down a flight of stairs. I'd had to pay a therapist to find someone to ask me questions like that. But I recovered and offered the all-American, all-purpose defense for ill feelings of the spirit, "Oh, I'm just a little tired is all." It took every ounce of will to get away from him and into the safety of my car to let my body wail, and another three years to tell him and the rest of my colleagues that I was living with HIV.

We finally arrive at one of the tributaries of the Mekong, albeit after our taxi runs out of gas, and board the ferry at My Tho. The sun begins its decline, and there is a golden patina to the land and the buildings, giving the massive river a mythical glow that matches its name in Vietnamese: *Cuu Long*, which Tuong tells me means: "Forever Life of the Dragon." Indeed, the Mekong is one of the longest rivers in Asia, following its near 3000-mile path from its source in the mountains of western China through eastern Tibet to where it empties out into the delta of south Vietnam.

The ferry fills and we head at a diagonal across the muddy river. I look around at the children staring at me, absorbing all of my otherness with their eyes, reminding me of how mesmerized I was as a boy when I saw real Korean students from the Methodist college in my hometown in Indiana walk into the drugstore, stunned that their eyes were really eyes and their feet really feet. The tragedy of poverty, particularly in Asia, is that parents often must sacrifice their children, literally in order to survive. In Vietnam as elsewhere in Southeast Asia, children are used to fuel this faltering economy, sent off to cities by parents to be sold into brothels or to sort through trash to find scraps of metal to recycle. Though Vietnam has made strides in its economy, well over a third of its 78 million people live in a desperate poverty, which severely affects public health. I notice the baggage of the passengers: the baskets of fish, a tub of soap lard, spilled blood running in a rivulet from a package of meat, a new TV in a box, and, to my horror, a cage of young dogs on the back of a motorbike.

Tuong's brother has built a new house off a little highway, two floors with several bedrooms, airy and bright, a palace compared to most houses here. His whole family is here, those who stayed behind and live down a dirt road and those who work at Motorola in Atlanta and give pedicures in plush downtown hotels in Chicago. In the background Tuong's brother, whose English sounds no different from my 16-year-old nephew's, and his Vietnamese nephews are blasting hip-hop on the stereo and playing a video game on the TV. In the kitchen a pot of meat is brewing and Tuong's old buddies and brothers are drinking rice wine and singing Beatles songs in Vietnamese. Tuong's father, a former officer in the South Vietnamese Army and a prisoner for eight years, sits quietly, without any expression, in the other room. He'd come a long way since 1975, and so had Vietnam.

The next evening Tuong takes me to meet one of his child-hood friends who now presides as a monk over a small local temple, hidden in the thick trees off a dirt road near his brother's house. Surrounding the temple and its Buddhist statuary is a simple garden of flowering trees and shrubbery sculpted into the shapes of deer and elephants. We climb the tile steps up to the modest white temple where a fat laughing Lucky Buddha greets us at the door.

Inside there is an altar with a golden Buddha framed by two rustic portraits of two severe old monks. A large bell hangs from the ceiling. Landscapes of rivers and mountains are painted on the walls. Then, without a sound, out of a back room appears Tuong's old friend, the monk, Le Hong Thai. Le Hong wears a long, simply sewn white shirt with brown pants. He is small, birdlike, and, like many religious people I've met, has a kind of translucent quality not only to his skin but to his whole presence, making me feel a bit over-exposed. I can feel him studying me as he takes the gifts of fruit from my hands, places them in a bowl before the Buddha and slowly bows. We follow him to a small room, painted in a soothing light lime green. Like him and the whole temple and grounds, the room is polished and clean, simple and fresh. Le Hong brings us iced tea, and Tuong explains the purpose of our visit.

Le Hong folds his hands as he listens to Tuong's translations of my questions and then waits in silence until he finds his answers, which are delivered in a crisp, precise series of sing-song diphthon-gal notes that of course mean nothing to me. But the sounds of his voice and the movements of lips and hands express an emotion that I can hear and see with a clarity that mesmerizes and oddly calms me. I'd learned after several frustrating interviews those first weeks in India listening to women who'd been abandoned by their families and wrongfully blamed for their husbands' dying from AID that, even with a good translator, it was best for me to watch their faces and open my eyes as wide as possible, like a lens of a camera absorbing light, so as to do justice to the truth of their impassioned narratives.

"We have a Buddhist Association that helps the poor and the sick and the old," Le Hong informs us. Predictably, he explains that people are dissatisfied and that is why they turn to drugs and destroy themselves with desire for money and sex. Over the years Buddhism has been weakened in Vietnam by one after another of the great powers of the world, China, the Colonial French, the Catholic Church, the Japanese, and then of course us, the United States. But perhaps its greatest and oldest challenge has returned in the promise of globalization: the seductions of wealth and the material world.

Falling away from the practice of the *dharma* brings suffering, he reminds us with sincerity. "Right thinking brings right action," he says with a smile curling his lips ever so slightly. Then he says something a bit odd, or this is how I understand Tuong's translation. He says that HIV doesn't come from a scientific cause but from superstition. *Superstition?* After listening to him a bit longer, it dawns on me what he means: Superstition is any kind of false belief that leads to suffering. He's referring to the concept of "cause and effect" and the mercurial doctrine of *karma*.

"People are afraid for the future," he says. "They are confused and seduced by the new materialism that is coming with the money and the culture of foreigners." Le Hong's mouth is pursed with emotion. Tuong, who has filmed part of our conversation, now has his camera on his knees and is deep in thought. I wonder what he thinks about *karma*. I wonder too how this explanation of his old friend's would help Tuong's nephew who has fallen under the spell of heroin and has joined the thousands of young people seriously at risk of contracting HIV. At 16 he's already lost his three best friends in bizarre and tragic deaths due to the inescapable logic of addiction. The government's propaganda posters of ghostly monsters and comic book prostitutes have not saved them, nor have the teachings of the Buddhists.

But suddenly Le Hong leaps up from his chair and disappears behind a curtain into his tiny sleeping room. When he returns, he carries in his delicate hands a bracelet of dark orange beads. Le Hong smiles and hands me the beads. "Eighteen Buddhas for you," Tuong explains. "These are prayer beads for good luck and protection."

Then a boy appears in the doorway and the monk gets up and goes with him. We follow. A bell rings three times and the boy's chanting voice echoes in the temple and floats out into the garden, as ever so slightly he shakes three burning sticks of incense. The ceremony ends and I am filled with an overwhelming sense of sadness about what I don't know.

"I take a picture, take picture of you and Le Hong," Tuong
suggests, pushing me out onto the steps of the temple, and motion-
ing to Le Hong, who runs back inside to get a better robe. And
there we stand in front of the temple for Tuong's camera next to
the Lucky Buddha and the bush trimmed into the shape of a deer.

It is our fifth day in Ho Chi Minh City and our third following Pham Van on his tireless rounds about the city on his aging
motorbike as he nurtures and trains those most at risk for HIV:
sex workers, street youth, teenagers, and drug users. Pushing 60
but with the energy of a twenty-five-year-old, Pham Van is the true
communist, if there is such a thing. Trained back in the sixties by
American Unitarians to do social work, he has survived the last
thirty years in Saigon, teaching, acting, working as a journalist,
and then patiently working with the communist government to try
to make their dreams of being a self-sufficient society of workers
into a reality. Now after several years working for NGOs like
Save The Children and fed up with corrupt officials, he and his
wife, a retired high school English teacher, have devoted themselves to preventing the spread of HIV in the schools, the streets,
and the slums. "We make our house an open place," he told me
when we first met at our hotel. "They come for spend the night, to
take shower. We give them little bit of food, a clean shirt. And we
never worry if they steal anything." His English comes through a
kind of French-Vietnamese dialect and construction, but I hang on
every word even as we weave through thousands of bikes pouring
out into old Saigon's boulevards.
The day before, he took us to a community-based organiza-
tion in a claustrophobic slum of corrugated shanties run by women
determined to break the generational cycle of dependence on sex
work to pay for food and rent. He has helped them to band together and work on small income-generating projects. Their
children, who usually work sifting trash for metal and other
materials to recycle, swarm around Tuong and me as we make our
way through alleys no wider than a sidewalk. But after about an
hour of talking to the women who are all peeling onions for a
factory that makes soup mix, our stay is cut short when the police
became suspicious and threaten to take Tuong and his camera
away with them. Technically, we were supposed to have filed for
permission with the appropriate government officials to be able to

meet with organizations like Pham Van's. And as someone with HIV, I am of course not even allowed to be in the country. So quickly Pham Van gets us out of there.

It takes nearly an hour on the back of Pham Van and his son's motorbike to reach his weekly meeting with HIV drug-users. We cross back and forth over tributaries of the polluted Saigon River and through slums that hug the banks, until we come to a little outdoor café in a new quarter the government has set aside for a manufacturing zone.

"Bring more people," Pham Van implores this group as the meeting begins. "Helping others helps you."

The woman's pink t-shirt reads "Trends." Her shriveled body is a shell of bones with skin tightly wrapped around it. A gray pallor discolors her sad face. Her sunken eyes and hollow cheeks make her nose long and her head is too big for her frame. Her husband sits slumped next to her, a dingy white construction hat in his hands, and an expression on his face as if he is trapped in a body of pain. Across the table two men seethe in anger, arms folded, eyes narrowed to slits. A man hides under an Adidas cap. A child sits on a window ledge behind a mother with one eye, whose hands are folded in her lap. Pham Van tells me after the meeting that these drug-users go to this half-blind woman's food stall when they are sick and have no food. "She like a saint to them," he says. "We give her little money for their food."

I look around at their faces, as Pham Van is talking to them, suggesting they do some work or go walking together. And I wonder, why does he do this? "Every month they die," he told me. "Last month there was four, twenty-five already this year."

Tuong lights a cigarette out of nervousness and throws his pack onto the table to share with them. The world of drug-users and AIDS has a potent mythology in Vietnam as it does every-where in the world. Here, drug-users are known to attack the police and anyone who comes between them and their addiction, sticking needles in their arms to draw blood and then threatening to stab and infect whoever comes too close. Drugs, according to the government and UNAIDS, account for most of Vietnam's growing HIV population. Seventy percent of drug users in Ho Chi Minh City have been infected, adding to the long sad history of opium's effect on the Vietnamese, whose mountainous poor still use the drug as a way to deaden the despair of hunger. And it's not just the urban and rural poor; the government admits that at least 20 percent of those employed by the state have serious drug problems as well.

Smoke hangs in the heavy humid air. They take every drag deep into their lungs, sucking for what is left of the pleasure in their fading lives, falling into fits of coughing. Pham Van introduces us and Tuong translates, whispering as he leans toward me so that I can keep what little eye contact the group offers. Most say only a few words, look off, say something else, shrug, and the next takes his turn. I gather from Tuong that someone is missing. A couple of members shake their heads. "He got caught stealing," a man reports. "Stealing a bike," Tuong whispers, when I ask what he stole, trying to write it all down. This bicycle story actually brings a few smiles to their faces. The following day, however, I learn that the man was missing not because of stealing a bike, but because he was dead.

A waiter sets sodas before us, brightening the gloom. Rain clouds smudge the afternoon sun. Behind the café, to my surprise, is a tennis court, bright green, white stripes, but empty.

The husband with the construction cap now speaks. He speaks almost as if I am the only one present, imploring me to understand, his face and body reminiscent of those tiny crucifixes you see on hiking trails in the mountains in Italy. Tuong listens very carefully, translating what he can: "He says the government makes the HIV people attend meetings each month, to check on them, and if they don't go they are taken to jail. He collects trash, pushes a wheelbarrow around all day. His job is all he and his wife have and it makes him feel better when he works. He don't know what he will do if he lose his job." While the husband speaks, I steal glances at his frail wife beside him, watching her breathe. I am drawn to her body, the deep eye sockets, the black needle stains up and down her arms, but mostly it is the mechanical rise and fall of her breath that upstages the drama of her husband's heartbreaking account of their life. Each time her chest collapses in its exhale, I wait in sympathetic terror holding my own breath, thinking that it will be her last. But then up again comes a spurt of life, laboriously her lungs draw in more air, though they are so weak she has to massage her nostrils to get in more oxygen. It is so painful to watch that I find myself breathing more deeply, expanding my lungs, hoping somehow it is helping her. In my mind I have a macabre image of wrapping myself around her frail body and trying to breathe into her, pumping her emaciated body back to life. As I watch her breathe, I recall standing over my grandfather's disappearing body as he lay in the VA hospital dying of emphysema. Pham Van tells me after the meeting that he doesn't know how she has stayed alive as long as she has. "Some go quickly. The young go very fast. But others, like her, they go on and on, nobody know why."

With the permission of Pham Van and the group, Tuong circles around the table as they talk, taking photos even as he translates. I watch him as he sets up his shots, sensitively focusing on their faces, moving in close and then back away, as if he is not taking a photograph but rather offering his respect, his acknowledgment of their suffering. Photography for Tuong has become a way to express what he can't in English, as he told me once in his basement apartment. "I start to take more and more when I come to America. With my photographs I don't have to worry if people understand me. I can communicate the things I feel without speaking." With a camera around his neck, he became possessed, and now I understood how he'd lost part of his hearing photographing the traditional dragon dance during Chicago's Chinese New Year when a firecracker exploded in his ear.

Everywhere we go he takes pictures: of street children selling lottery tickets, old women selling fish, shoeshine boys, men sleeping in their trash carts, funeral processions passing our hotel. Even at Vietnam's War Remnants Museum, a museum of photographs, he took pictures, hundreds of them. The museum has the opposite effect on me, driving me literally into the courtyard after only an hour of viewing napalm bombs exploding over villages, fires engulfing huge swaths of rice fields, mangled piles of blood-soaked women and children fleeing the infamous village of My Lai. But worst of all are the photographs of the genetically deformed children (even several in jars of formaldehyde), who are still being born with little wings for arms and flippers for feet, due to Agent Orange seeping through the earth into village water supplies. The real heroes of the war, one learns, when you watch a war unfold in the cold shadows of these black and white photos, are those who gave their lives to magnify the horror and hubris of that "dirty war" that consumed the lives of fifty-eight thousand GIs and over three million Vietnamese. Like a shrine, a whole wall was covered with portraits of correspondents, from Japan, Vietnam, Australia, Britain, and of course America. I watched him as he photographed the last photos in these journalists' cameras before they were killed, in awe of them and what was before him: A career he so desperately wants and a past he can never have back.

When everyone else has had a chance to speak, Pham Van turns to me and asks, "Do you want to speak now?"

I am scribbling furiously, trying to catch up with my note taking, but really it is a stalling tactic. What can I possibly say to them? Ever since sitting down in this café, I've found myself trying to hide my health by contracting my body, hunching over, crawling into the black ink scratchings in my notebook.

Tuong looks at me and pleads, "Please, Michael, speak slow, okay?" At least, I think, it will be his words and not mine. How absurd it all has become, I think: America destroying Vietnam only to build it back up with tourist money. Fifteen-year-old girls from poor rice farms selling themselves to fat Germans who'd throw their own daughters out of the house if they got caught having sex with their boyfriends. Drug addicts shooting heroin to stay alive. Tuong telling dying people who have nothing that this white guy, his teacher, tried to kill himself by sleeping with another man because he is too ashamed to admit that he finds pleasure in the embrace of another human being. I have acted in Beckett plays in college, and I have always imagined that those worlds of his were abstractions of reality. Now I see that they are not abstractions. Godot is back in the city at the ice cream shop where we met the day before a sixteen-year-old boy who wanted to be called, of course, Michael—after Michael Jackson—a street kid, who spoke nearly flawless English and who had open sores up and down his arms and legs, and whose alcoholic father, who works at a factory that makes Mickey Mouse dolls, beats him if he steps foot in their one room apartment when he comes to give his mother some money from shining shoes on the streets. The lunacy of what I am feeling is not a joke, but a way to trick oneself out of the trap of getting caught thinking too much. "You can't think about it. You have to just embrace it," a friend of mine once told me, who'd been positive much longer than I have. So I open my mouth and try not to think as I tell my story.

And at one point I hold up my notebook, showing them what I am doing and telling them it is their book, too. "Our book," I say like I am some kind of politician. But that doesn't have much effect on them until Tuong says something, something on his own, something about me that makes his lip quiver. What, I never find out, but after he does, they seem to lean in toward me waiting for what I have to say.

Pham Van suggests they ask me questions. A man who hasn't said much asks very politely if I am sure I have HIV because it doesn't look like I am sick. A common question I've been asked from South Africa to India, because when someone there has to finally admit that they have HIV, their life is nearly over. Pham Van explains that I do Yoga, intelligently emphasizing how I am taking care of my body rather than the fact that I have access to drug treatments, which they do not. Intrigued by this mention of Yoga, the group breaks into a debate over just exactly what Yoga is.

The next question, though, throws me. "They want to know how you got it?" Tuong reluctantly says from the other side of the table.

I know what I have to say—what I have to admit, something even drug-users in a traditional culture like Vietnam can find offensive—that I have contracted HIV from having sex with another man. In a way it is a test. I have to tell the truth. I swallow and the image comes to me of my apartment in Chicago and the drunken, drugged nights I have shared with nameless men, angry and lonely like me. So I tell them: "I had sex with men. I drank. I did drugs, too. Sometimes, I wanted to kill myself."

But they still aren't satisfied. I look around and they are all looking my way, even those who have kept their heads down. "What happened when you found out?" a man in the corner asks. Again memories circle around in my head, memories that seem fresher than ever. I can feel my throat and the discomfort in my body as I shift and squirm. I remember the clinic and the room in which I was told and the indifference in the voice of the woman behind the desk: "You weren't expecting this, were you?" I see myself naked in the shower wanting to pound my fist through the bathroom wall. "I was angry," I tell them, my right hand unconsciously forming into a clenched fist under the table. "At who?" Tuong asks instinctively, not necessarily for them but for himself.

"I was angry at the world." I tell him, my fist now rising out from under the table. I look at Pham Van and he is nodding, as he must have nodded at words like these many, many times before.

I look at Tuong in a way I never have before. In his face, I can see now my own, a frustrated foreigner unable to speak, like the hundreds of immigrant students who have sat in classes before me, not simply desperate for the knowledge of how to put words in the agreed-upon order, but desperate to be translated out of the past into the language of the future.

I look around at these people, their gray bodies already losing the color of life, and on their faces, to my astonishment, I can see compassion. They aren't dragging me down with them, which is what I believed they had been trying to do; no, they seem to want to donate to me what belief they have left in the value of life.

"I don't want to die," I finally say, doing everything I can not to fall apart. Tuong whispers my words and when I look up it appears that their faces have left their bodies and come within inches of my eyes. "I want to make more people understand what this disease is . . . that is why I came here . . . I don't want anyone else to have to feel the shame that I have." Tuong nods and then offers his translation. Up from out of his brown body and lips come my words, my loss. I listen to his Vietnamese voice and the emotions riding the waves of his diphthongal glides, and as I do, I realize that what I have said, what experiences I believe are mine and mine alone, are not really mine at all.

Then a man asks about the origins of AIDS. I try to get across the African monkey theory, but they aren't having any of it. He believes it comes from America.

When the meeting is over, there is an awkward shuffling around. They walk away slowly. But something feels incomplete. I want to shake someone's hand, I want to touch them, hug someone. I walk up behind the fragile woman with the pink t-shirt, who leans on her husband as they hobble to the road. She raises her head to look at me but then it sinks back to watching her feet so as not to fall. Then without speaking, I put my arm around her shoulder. It feels like I have placed a log on a dying flower. She turns and looks up, smiles and then, embarrassed, buries her head into her chest.

As we climb onto our motorbikes, dark clouds sink over the streets and soon it begins to rain. Pham Van worries that I might catch a cold and stops to buy me a cheap plastic poncho, but as we are buying it, the rain begins to pour so we run into a tailor's shop.

The rain sweeps over the city and soon the owner's wife gets up from her sewing machine and finds two small wooden stools. And we sit there, Pham Van and I, watching the rain and the children playing in the downpour. I learn that Pham Van in his spare time writes lyrics to folk songs. He tells me about plays he has directed and puppet shows, too. "I like the puppets," he tells me, smiling. And he tells me of how difficult it is sometimes for him to become so close to so many people only to know that they will soon pass away. "Young people," he sighs. "They die too quickly. I have to take their pictures. We go to the picnic, we make the party. I think they need this so much. And then I take my camera. I take the photo with the happy faces. Because when they die, they have to have a picture for the funeral . . . for us to remember them. We tell them we support the end day. It is important for them to know . . . that they will not die alone. I know they will die soon, so I take their photo. But sometimes I don't take them in time. Some die, no picture. A couple of weeks ago a boy die, a good boy, who was working with us as the peer counselor, but he loved the drugs too much. That night someone call and tell me. I couldn't sleep. . . . I couldn't because I don't have a picture. So I just write down everything he told me about his life. I write and I write . . . the secrets, the stories, all the things I remember he told me. Then I go back to sleep."

LAURA CASTELLANOS

We Were School Children

Speeding back from HaLong Bay at dusk we saw a line of children
and we asked them where are you going
carrying their chairs home from school. Hard plastic patio chairs
in rose or green that can hold a scratch bumped between blue
asphalt and yellow fields until the children were picked off
like ducks to the pond or lawyers to court
by squat cinder squares with television antennas.

Back on my ranch, the 8 yr. old brother of the 6 yr. old daughter had
       broken open
the 10 lb. bag of flour. They wanted to go to school so they made
       themselves white.
Their parents want to know if I think they have a case.

In Hanoi I have a case of Coltrane among the French Colonial
       Communist redux
of high white arches with vines and clotheslines for throwback music
and muted soccer on television they at least acknowledge is state-run.
The man at the next table politely waits until the set is done
to inquire if we're Americans. Then asks if we need help with our
       election.
Bicycles pinball through streets indifferent to every victor
as we dodge along home. Little doggies.

On my family's first Motorola I watched Cronkite every night and kept
       a tally
of their dead, our dead and the MIA whose bracelet I could wear.
We grew up to be a kind and gentle people singing for our lives in big
       cars.

PHILIP PARDI

Call and Response

Just one thing dreams of returning as itself: the hands.

❋

Never mind winter will be mild.

Never mind the dumpster is forever spilling.

A squirrel prays to god the way god must sometimes pray
        to a squirrel: don't, don't, please, don't. . .

Flattened. The tail, quivering.

❋

You may be surprised by the speed at which decisions
are made for you.

You'll be excused if, reaching down for what you want, you kick it
just out of reach.

What if you escape, but escape back
                             into this same garment?

A meeting at the crossroads of water and water.
Boots for excellently crossing small streams,
                          urns for pouring.

What if it fits, the footsteps spaced perfectly for your stride?

❋

On the radio, a man hears the *Star-Spangled Banner* from Hanoi.
Chance of rain today: 100%.
Morning, perforation.
The way water embraces itself is the revelation.

147

The man thinks of thieves spooning honey onto roses, running razors into tea
        bags, of what he'll do when his last pair of shoes is wet through, why
        there's always something between him and his idea of what's missing.
Two flies, trapped between window and screen, froze overnight.
The Vietnamese military band plays the anthem perfectly.
The man never liked that song, never liked the word "ramparts."
Perhaps, he thinks, there's a mathematical function we've yet to invent, the
        precise algebraic formulation of *caressing*.
Chance of rain today, 100%.
The way an eggshell hides its soul till the revelation shatters it
        is the revelation.
From his front step, the man eyes newspapers drowned on sidewalks: this
        he likes, the news as landscape.
He longs to do for his feet what prayer does for the hands.
On the road, he can't see it, but he knows one bus driver has just waved
        to another.

⁕

Each year, in the autumn, we visit the old house. We meet the new owners, if
they are new, and walk through the garden, if they let us. Perhaps a plant
needs pruning, or the fence a nail. We talk with them, explain the way water
can rise quickly from the culvert, show them the spring in the lower meadow.
And then we broach the issue of ashes.

⁕

Rain, and the robins descend
and get to work
or is this their joy, their rapture?

Wet leaves, wet stones, wet skin, I listen, am listened to.
A marsh hawk unfolds, white-rumped and listing
left, lifting itself into hackberry limbs.

There is nothing that is not falling from us,
nothing we do
that isn't a grabbing.

⁕

Sometimes, watching you

148

from afar
        the same urge
I feel amidst hemlocks
when a rare redstart comes near:
be still, raise eyes slowly
                go over
each aspect of wing, throat, limb
                    press it hard

into memory.

           *

Beneath the hum
of delay

a hand gathers,

ungathers:
the ebb and flow of the I.

There's always one sound

taking its place
behind another

always a small plane

circling, circling.
Beneath it all, trees

and elegies: *This*

is how it happens. First
you forget to be yourself.

Then you get used to it.

           *

All these years I would see them and make a wish. "Hawks for good luck," we used to say. But I don't know what it means now that you tell me they're actually vultures. The head gives them away, you say. What does it mean to wish on a vulture? Do you think they—the ones I meant to pray to—knew what I meant?

✿

"When we behold a wide, turf-covered expanse,
we should remember that its smoothness
is mainly due to the inequalities
having been slowly leveled by worms.

It is a marvelous reflection that
the whole of the superficial mould over
any such expanse has passed, and will
again pass, every few years, through

the bodies of worms. The plough is one
of the most ancient and most valuable
of man's inventions; but long before
he existed the land was in fact regularly

ploughed, and still continues to be thus ploughed
by earthworms."
                    Thus Darwin, late in life, looked ahead.

LÝ HỒNG ANH

Hair and Homeland

Rang va toc la goc con nguoi.
Teeth and hair are a person's cornerstone.
—Old Vietnamese Proverb

The wig wasn't altogether ugly. It was too ordinary-looking, too Mary Tyler Moore. I would have preferred for it to be blue or orange if it was going to pretend to be something it wasn't. The color was actually identical to my old hair. To me, it was a badge of cowardice, regardless of the shade.

In the end, I put aside my stubbornness and wore it. Only once, partly out of guilt, partly out of obligation.

I could have looked much worse. There is an old-world remedy for skin abrasions—fresh turmeric root. Peeled, then rubbed directly on the painful wounds on my face, it stained my skin, clothes and pillowcase a bright indignant yellow. The nurses were the first ones to apply it for me in the hospital in Vietnam. The smell of it was sharp and spicy, reminding me of curries and fish, and later of the intensive care unit where I smelled it under the hands of the women who told me that it would make me beautiful again. My family often says I owe it to turmeric that my face was not permanently ruined. The fluorescent stains on my skin faded soon enough, more quickly than the memories of how I looked while I was healing.

The Vietnam I knew about from stories told in America was more intriguing to me than it was treacherous. The decision to go was simple. I needed to see the other side, worlds away, in order to find truth in what I already know. But my family panicked when I told them I was going to "go home" to their homeland, a country I'd never known and they hadn't known for the latter half of their lives. Further, I was to examine the unfamiliar north, not just the central and south from which my family came. Despite their disapproval, my family was the very reason why I went.

All my explanations about why I wanted to go and why I wanted to stay took place before my first year in Vietnam was over, before I had my terrible accident in a heavy tropical rain shower on a Honda Super Cub motorbike, smack in a busy Hanoi intersection.

The two countryside women on their bicycle, unaccustomed to one-way streets and fast-moving motorbikes, and I, unaccustomed to erratic vehicles turning corners onto the wrong lane, collided head-on. Of the women, one suffered bruises, and the other a fractured jaw. I was injured severely with an epidural hematoma—a blood clot that caused my brain to swell, impairing my breathing and rendering me comatose.

A pedaling *xich lo* driver was my ambulance. I had been on my way to pick up my childhood friend who was coming to visit me from overseas. With the help of another *xich lo* driver, she cleverly managed to track me down at the hospital when I didn't show. She was the first on the scene, and my mother likes to tell the story about how my dear friend spotted and recognized my feet first, like you can with corpses, I imagine, and that I owe all the ensuing swift medical action to my distinctive feet. The surgeons, experts in head trauma, effectively performed the same operation for nine other helmet-less victims that day without the use of any CAT-scans, just as doctors did day after day, in hospital after hospital throughout the country.

My family was probably more traumatized than I was. While I was able to absolve myself of responsibility, they couldn't. "We never should have let her go," they lamented.

I might have spared myself all those nights in Viet Duc Hospital. I wouldn't have had to come home to the U.S. in a wheelchair, an eighty-pound, thirty-six-kilo shadow of myself. I would have avoided having to hear my relatives' confirmations of their paranoid communist-assassin-attempts-against-overseas-Vietnamese-a.k.a.-former-enemies theories. I would still have had a full head of hair, long sheets of brown-black silk, perceived by others to be my ultimate asset as a young, desirable woman. My visit would not have been a mistake in my family's eyes.

I never had any regrets about that year. The way I saw it, I was going to my ancestral land, the place of my mother tongue, the womb of my existence, a place with new lessons to be learned. I knew of the perilous exodus of refugees after the war, and I understood that it had once been a dangerous place for the older members of my community, but I still wanted to see the reunified republic for myself. In my short lifetime, I had very little emotional baggage to pack for the journey.

I wanted to know if all Vietnamese, not just the ones who live overseas, believe that blood-ties run as deep as a bottomless well; if any of us ever get bored with eating rice; if we are all unfailingly late for every gathering; or if we always are barefoot or wear plastic slippers instead of shoes. The list goes on. . . . I wanted to study the language and unravel my own personal mysteries for a year.

By the time the accident happened, nine months after my arrival, I was in no position to explain anything. I slept undisturbed in a coma for three days. The third day, my first memory was the horrible gagging when the ventilator tube was removed, my hands tied to the bed to prevent me from ripping out the remaining tubes and wires in my panic. I was confused by the jump in time from driving my motorbike to lying in a hospital bed, physically unable to form the words to ask what happened. When given a pen and paper by my friends, I couldn't write anything with my writing hand because the left side of my body was temporarily paralyzed. Later my father rushed into the hospital room with my mother, straight from the airport, and took my bandaged head in his arms, sobbing with relief that I was alive. My mother, jetlagged, held my IV-ed hand at the bedside all day, as if her grip could keep me from flying away again.

I knew I had to go back to the States for further medical care but I asked my parents, teary-eyed, my speech slurred, to promise they would let me come to Vietnam again after I was well. They looked at my face, all black and blue, cut up and stitched, and with the most tremendous love I have ever known, agreed to let me return. Three months later, I did, to everyone's disbelief.

For me, the most regrettable part of my accident, apart from the countless hours of strain and worry on my family, was that I had to leave before I was ready. For my family, the most regrettable circumstance seemed to be my scarred shaven head. "She used to be so pretty," my grandmother said. I was unexpectedly home to attend a big friends-of-family wedding that spring, the shockingly bald veteran after my tour of duty in Nam. "Your parents will be so ashamed," she said.

At the hospital they first chopped my hair off with scissors. Before I'd worn it down; it covered my shoulders and breasts — infinitely lustrous and feminine-looking. I'd always thought the longer the better, and had never trimmed it much. Each long bunch must have been gathered, snipped, and piled on the metal tray on the trolley next to the stretcher. The pile grew higher and higher, my thick straight dark strands remaining in obedient rows, limp with defeat. How strange they must have looked detached from my body. Did they still look beautiful then? Now my head, with only strong spikes and uneven pieces left, was ready for the clippers.

"What a waste—such smooth soft hair," the nurse might have said, turning my head to one side to finish prepping me for surgery.

Had I been awake, the little bits of hair would have prickled my neck, the teeth of the electric clippers hitting my mop with one spine-rattling buzz after another. The hospital floor was scattered with a landscape from my youth. In America, whenever my uncle was cutting our hair in the kitchen, we children would pretend that the black accumulations on the linoleum were mutant rodents from an alien planet who had come to see what human feet taste like. We would shriek and stamp on the mounds while my father would chastise us and say we were making a mess. Getting down on hands and knees, we'd push the piles around, arranging new enemies to continue our game, while the next cousin got his hair trimmed, then the next.

After I was released from the hospital, I was pleased to discover that my head was actually nicely shaped. It felt trendy cool, like I should pierce some extra body parts, besides my ears, for the full effect. The long pronounced sear that ran along the side of my head like a baseball stitch just fueled my idea that I looked like a real badass. The first few months of my recovery, I thoroughly enjoyed the mischievous lightness of it. I found great satisfaction in rubbing my head and even encouraged others to rub it whenever they admired my new look. I would strut into my physical therapist's office, beaming and tall, never the least bit embarrassed. I felt like I had won a dare. When the whiffle started to grow, I was disappointed, and even now, I sometimes miss the suggestive curves and carefree smoothness of my hairlessness.

Two years after the crash, my family discovered in a fortune told at the time of my birth that a significant danger would be caused by moving vehicles during my twenty-fourth year, but that my survival would be ensured by the presence of a particular shining star. Everyone is predisposed to adversity or calamity during his or her birth year (every twelve years on the eastern zodiac) so what happened to me could have been expected. Before I was out of the hospital, my aunts, uncles, parents, and grandparents had prayed nightly to the ancestors asking them to spare my life though they later admitted that prayers might be futile—nearly everything is predestined. "When you don't know what else to do,

154

you beg," one older auntie had said.

Four days before the wedding, my first big public appearance after the incident, I was trying on dresses to decide which one wouldn't make my emaciated body look too skinny. I was pulling off a white silk dress over my head and thinking to myself, not white, it's too pathetic, too virginal, when one of my younger aunties—the family's speaks-her-mind—burst into my room. She was the one who'd been in charge of the wig purchase.

"So what? You lose your hair, but you're okay. No reason to make everyone feel sorry for you. You want everybody to look at your head and feel sorry for you, huh?" she demanded, "Well, sometimes you have to do something you don't want to do, just to make some old people happy. Stop being selfish—wear the wig—it's a good quality one!"

"I just want to be myself. They all know already—what's the point of pretending everything is okay when it's not? I'm not ashamed," I countered. "Besides, that thing looks like a dead animal! I won't wear it—you can't make me!" Nevertheless, deep inside I knew that it is impossible to debate filial piety issues that are dozens of generations old. When you do choose to put up a fight, you just bite your lip, close your eyes, and throw your fists in the air to see if they do anything.

The life of an Asian woman who exerts her free will within her family can be a fine balancing act—maintaining your independence and personal integrity, while doing as much as you can to look self-sacrificing. Delicate punches if you swing.

With love comes duty, and with duty comes sacrifice. I hated to admit it, but the obedient accommodating girl deep inside me still chanted this mantra, despite my fierce insistence that there was nothing embarrassing about my appearance. I had thought that always wanting-to-please girl was dead and buried, after an adolescent victory, the mourning period long over—but I was wrong.

Grown woman of the world that I imagined myself to be, I eventually agreed to wear the wig, if not for my sake, then for the venerable honor of my idiosyncratic family. It was the first and only time I ever wore it.

I don't know why they believed that they would be able to fool four hundred of their closest friends and family. Though really, it wasn't an exercise in kidding anyone. It was a way of saying that we won't tell you about it, and you'll have nothing to ask, because we've made everything look normal. By the end of the day, nearly everyone at the reception knew about my trip, my head and my wig. "Poor girl," they said among themselves, "she probably could have gotten married soon too." Then to my face, "You should come back to the States to live—so full of opportunities. What can you do over there anyway? It's so backward, so poor. It's a dangerous place—come home to where you belong."

I would nod politely and smile, fingering the wig to make sure it wasn't out of place, and say, "It's different now and changing more every day. I love my life there." I wasn't going to convince everyone of my perspective, but it was important to try. I understood that decades of struggling with loss and sorrow would not soon be forgotten. I knew I was no hero, but my hope was to loosen things up a little and make room for new ideas, a new history that mixed the good with the bad.

When we stopped by to visit my ever-gentlemanly grandfather later the same day, he informed me that he had read in his most recent copy of *Paris Match* that even Elizabeth Taylor appeared in public after having her head shaved for brain surgery. He grinned at me and gave my hand a squeeze. I sat in my fine-tailored *ao dai* in his sunny house, with the wig in my lap, cool and relaxed now that I'd taken it off, and beamed at him. He told my parents, brother, uncle, and cousins, who happened to be in the living room, that even a famous movie star was in the same condition I was. And we were both still good-looking, he said, proudly pointing to the smiling pictures of her in the magazine twice, then turning his rosy convincing finger to point at me.

I was given a new life, another chance. After the stitches came out, I began to look like my old self again. Everyone said that they found me livelier and more outgoing than before. I had vital surges of energy as never before.

However, even years after the accident, after I had recovered into a more robust version of who I was before it happened, some people would still pity me. I'd decided to keep my hair short. Vietnamese friends and family, who had forgotten how quickly time passes, would squint their eyes and ask me inanely, "Your hair is taking a long time to grow, isn't it?" Perhaps when there's a fixed image of who you are or who you should be, any changes seem temporary. The same can be said of their beloved native soil, drastically different in the present day, yet forever frozen in the image of its younger or better days.

For years to follow, I kept returning to the place of my accident, the country from which they had fled and thought I ought also to flee. As I boarded flight after flight to Southeast Asia, my family would insist that I'd be better off elsewhere.

I like my hair short as much as I liked it long, and I understand more clearly how some wounds heal and others don't. To my mother's dismay, the controversial hairpiece has sat, since that day, in a box under my bed, like a throwaway consolation prize. Their love for me made them urge me to wear it. It was mostly out of love for them that I learned to love being Vietnamese and who I am.

These days you never see my scars anyway, not unless I show them to you. And my aunties can't disapprove anymore, not because I'm too old—I'll never be old enough not to have to listen to them—but because my hair has grown and I am no longer a visible victim of tragedy.

A friend who came to see me at the hospital the first few days after my surgery posed the question, "What happened to all your lovely hair?"

I assumed this was a rhetorical question, my head whistle clean. "Didn't you sell it?" she pursued.

The thought had actually never occurred to me, even though I was fully aware that no "trash" went to waste. Old used plastic sandals, cardboard pieces, pots and pans with the bottoms rusted out, even kitchen slop could always be sold to scavengers—who will pick through your garbage even if you don't.

My friend went on a mission, determined to corner the person who'd made a profit at the hands of my loss. "Someone else sold it for sure. Those thieves!" she hissed.

I wasn't upset in the least and was even comforted by the thought that my loss could have turned into at least somebody's fortune: the woman who sold it—an underpaid nurse or janitor— and the woman who is presently going around wearing my glorious locks as if they were her own. Just so I don't get too nostalgic about it, I assure myself that they probably look better on her. I sometimes see a Vietnamese woman ahead of me among the motorbike traffic with a shiny black bob or coifed bun that is a little conspicuous looking. I'll pull up right next to her and catch myself craning my neck, trying to spy an artificial hairline.

It would be satisfying to see another part of myself reincarnated, resilient and carrying on in the flow of things.

Mark Weiss, photograph

Beyond

DIANE SHIPLEY DeCILLIS

Childhood Revisited as a Musical

Debussy's *Claire de Lune* and me
 lying beneath an oak in the yard
stunned by its stature, especially from this

worm's-eye view, searching beyond the nest
 of branches, that I might discover
something personal in the sky,

its fleece of clouds traveling,
 like the commercials urging us,
with the sincerity of a jingle, to *fly*.

The clouds, postcards from distant lands,
 saying, *This universe is so gigantic*,
the possibilities of being rescued

are endless!
 But this is the prelude, I think as I look
at Sittu, my Lebanese grandmother

who, like her mother, regards the males
 of our family with the reverence
of Handel's *Messiah*

and me with disdain, like a baritone note
 held in a tragic opera,
just for having this DNA. After all,

she helped direct this double X
 chromosomal character. Was I wrong
to want to wear a petticoat and sing

I enjoy being a girl,
 or to imagine I was Audrey Hepburn
All I want is a room somewhere . . .

that I'll be discovered for the flower
    I am? And yet,
there were lyrical notes, contrapuntal.

Even with her Greek chorus of fates
    and furies, when the jaunty themes from
I Love Lucy and *Red Skelton* came on,

Sittu dropped her mask of tragedy,
    laughed with vaudevillian abandon.
I could barely watch the shows, watching her

holding her stomach, covering her mouth, trying
    to contain those natural improvisations —thinking,
there are roles inside that woman, aching to be played.

Looking for Stephen Dunn

You told us not to do it,
not to write about something
we really love, are too close to.
The fictive, you say (great word),

adds interest. To write intimate
truth is difficult, too much at stake,
but then you said,

finally the personal is all that matters,
we spend years describing stones,
chairs, abandoned farmhouses —
until we're ready.

Well, I think I'm ready.
That is to say,
I'm in love with you.
I discovered this at your last reading.

Sure, you're balding,
a little pudgy in the Pulitzer
with your white shirt and
professorial vest,

but the way you read your poetry,
the way you recite your lies,
is sexy.

It's as if you're reading to me
and I could imagine walking up to you,
throwing down your New & Selected
and taking you to an abandoned farmhouse
where I'd show you a few
of my best metaphors.

You might say I'm not ready,
that it's a mistake to force
the facile connection between art
and life.

But until I find it,
at least let me be relevant,
a small measure toward
that poem of simple truth.

D. M. FERGUSON

Back Home, At Night

That glinting, braided curtain of insect buzz,
that chitined mathematics encoding the pasture,
is more than cicadas or crickets, but what?
I don't know. But I do know the screech owls
who snag the silver line of adrenaline, shrieking,

"This is real!" while Dad wishes the farm
away, wishes his black flint arrowheads
(how sharp half-circles can be!), his scrapers,
his axe heads, everything his plow has pulled
from the earth, still breathed, maybe

in the hands of his grandsons whose feet
are pricked by the dry, sharp grass, eyes
by the dry, sharp stars, unable to blink,
because of the Milky Way, because
of the noise, because this is real.

MELISSA KOOSMANN

Fashion Show

The kids run through
the sprinkler, playing tag
in bright swimsuits.

The youngest pulls away, sick of losing,
and wraps herself
in a blue towel. She raises her skinny arms
and does a dance.

"I'm a model," she says, adjusting
the towel so
it's a gown.

She swings her hips, pacing
back and forth
by the plum tree, then flings
the gown away.

She props a bare foot
on a tree stump and puffs out her flat
gooseflesh chest.

The older kids laugh and imitate.
Pleased, the girl
strips off
her swimsuit,
slowly

the way she dimly knows
it must be done.

One boy groans
and hides his eyes.
"Put that back on," her brother says.

The little girl shakes her head
and wiggles. "Put that back on."
Her hands fall firm
on her hips. Her back curves.
How new this is.

GARY J. MAGGIO

Not Just the Thing, but the Idea of the Thing

It was Christmas Eve
and I just had an argument in my own house
with my second brother, who's the one
with the wife
who tortures their child.
My brother drinks
and I can't say anything until I drink
and the wine is. . .
not so good,

not just mixing with my cold blood but
the warm idea of it, wine at Christmas.
It makes me cry, him defending her
and my husband looking at me helpless
and his arms wrapped around our daughter's
whose nose is wrinkled by our yelling and
whose eyes rise to the tree lights
while her hands wrap so tightly around his fingers

I can't even look.
I blame my house for it,
not being big enough to accept my family;
not just for the rooms and the awful, wrong furniture
but for not having a heartbeat like a living thing.

And it wasn't like that when I was a child;
whatever the argument,
whatever the tortures I imagined,
no matter how helpless my brothers and I felt
in the limpness of the quiet,
That house, our childhood
Swallowed us in safety like warm scotch-breath from old lips.

Regent of Breath

All the time he was getting sicker
losing hope
I thought it was the old smoking
I thought it was the old voice

that says "I can't"
I thought it was that
mirror you hear about
You look into it one day

and see only a shadow
I thought it was the old legs that
in old age were
the best part of him

finding new support
shoes and hose, walking the
malls, moving ever
forward with light steps

On his toes
the uprush of
blood to his hips
to his conducting arms

to his smile
I thought the
lungs slowed the
will stopped the

legs killed the
smile
I thought I was
the helper the watcher

the regent of breath
until breath stopped
I thought it was
all about him

as I stood hard beside him but
I think he must have
grown tired of waiting
for me to soften.

WILLIS BARNSTONE

A child's Christmas in Manhattan

I snap a photo of the soul. It comes
out bedlam blue, reaching the snowball sky
of childhood where we are cutthroat bums
at ice war. Kids smack ice balls in your eye.
We blinded sledders burn way down the snow
gully, swerving a skid away from the third rail
sizzling deadly behind a barrier low
over the Hudson River's poisoned pail
of dead fish, condoms, and gray battleships
chatting of war in Asia. In our snow war
I take my hits on the way up. I duck
and fling my bombs. My frozen nose and lips
get whacked. Holy night, soul in Labrador,
I limp to mom's supper to get unstuck.

Our New York skyline in the 1930s now on fire in September

We faced the park and sometimes a big swan
over Manhattan rose from the small lake
where I went with my dad to row and scan
the New York skyline. Once a year mom took
a glass filled with pale wax and lit the wick,
her hands hovering over it like a well
she fell into. She wasn't weird or sick
but I didn't get it and broke her spell
with kid talk. Whispering for her dead, a Jew
for a few days, she never could parade
her feelings. Tonight I got myself to stand on
the street recalling mom's tall skyline that
had no Twin Towers then, nor now. Some prayed.
I slipped out awkwardly alone. All I could do
was let a candle burn out for those gone —
a girl in the plane flaming where she sat.

ERIC GOODMAN

Sleeper

When I was young, I killed someone. We were playing tackle in John's yard, and his team was winning. John's team usually won no matter the game or competition, for he was one of those rare, gifted boys, tall and sinewy, with an easy smile and what girls we knew called lover's eyes, although none of us, not even John, had yet spent the night in a girl's bed.

It was a Saturday in early spring, warm enough that we were playing in shirts and shorts. John's team had the ball. There had been an interception, and I was angry because it was my fault. We played three on three, but I can't remember another name except Rob Reilly, the only member of our group who had chest hair. Everyone else, including John, was smooth as a girl.

John was playing quarterback; I was rushing. One of his teammates snapped the ball. I counted to three while the receivers raced downfield. John feinted right then broke left, as he'd been doing all game, running towards the sideline marked by a thick-barked sugar maple. This time, although he was faster than I was, I refused to let him circle me. And perhaps because I was still pissed about the interception, I didn't just knock him out of bounds. I left my feet, shoulder aimed at his long torso. For a moment, I hung weightless, an assassin. Then my shoulder smacked John's gut, the best tackle I'd ever make, I knew it even as we flipped backwards. John landed back and head down with my weight on top of him. Instead of bouncing up and laughing—*Good hit*, is what he should have been saying; *great hit for a pussy like you*—there was a sound like a melon splitting open. For years we'd been running past the boulder beside the maple thinking nothing of it because it was out of bounds. Then John's head hit. I climbed off him. His lips were fixed and his eyes thrust open seeing something no one should ever see. Their light faded, fireflies smeared by an angry child, and I wanted to scream, *No, John, no!* for he'd always been a bit better than I was at everything, even goofing around. When we were nine or ten, John convinced me he'd eaten a butterfly, so I had to. After we caught one and I swallowed it whole, he burst out laughing. *Gotcha*. Then hairy Rob Reilly started to cry. After that, I don't remember exactly who did what.

That summer, while everyone else was getting ready for college, I was sent away. My parents knew this couple, Roger and Mary Bucholz, from my father's year in England, before I was born. Their daughter, Rachel, was nearly my age, and for reasons no one explained, it was agreed the Bucholz household—now in Ithaca, New York—was better equipped to deal with me than my own, where I'd lain around for the three months since it happened, wrapped in morbid conversations with John, twisting and disappearing in my grief. It was 1972, I was a virgin and a killer, although everyone assured me John's death was an accident and time healed all wounds, didn't I know?

I refused to let my parents drive me. They weren't about to give me their car, so on the Saturday morning of July 4th weekend, we drove to the Port Authority from Long Island, walked past the crazies back when 42nd Street really was 42nd Street, before it had been sanitized and Disneyed, and a mob of hookers and panhandlers rushed up to greet us. The whole scene so terrified my mother that she hung on my arm, although at that point I officially wasn't letting anyone touch me.

"Stan," she kept saying, "Stan," which was my father's name and mine, too. "I don't feel good about this."

We deposited my backpack in the silver belly of the Greyhound, and they waved goodbye. I refused to wave back because I was young and tortured and a killer and a virgin, etc.; because I had so much pain inside me I considered it my duty to share it around and who better to deputize than my parents whose greatest crime was to love me.

So they waved and I stared through them until the bus pulled out of the terminal headed for the Lincoln Tunnel and points north and west.

II.

Rachel Bucholz had straight brown hair she parted in the center and wore long and unadorned in the fashion of the day, except for black-eyed Susans inserted above her ears. She appeared each day in cut-offs and fringed tops or in one of several Mexican dresses, turquoise or purple, embroidered with yellow, red, white, and orange flowers. She wasn't home when I arrived and didn't bop in until sometime late the next morning. I was sitting on the screened porch overlooking the garden at the back of the house with her parents, Mary and Roger. Mary was small and British, a librarian of some sort, who wore her graying hair in a braid almost to her waist. Roger hummed Mozart and passed through life wearing a cheerful, principled grin, as if he had just heard a joke or parable he couldn't remember the words to. He had been born in Germany, the child of Jews who got him out in time, but died themselves. Roger and Mary met in England, then emigrated to the States after Roger, who was tall and kind and often seemed abstracted, made some discovery in quantum mechanics and was briefly in demand by American universities. Rachel was their youngest child, the only girl and the only one still at home, and perhaps because of the times, or because Roger had been one of the first anti-war professors at Cornell and encouraged free thinking, Rachel did pretty much what she wanted, no questions asked or answered.

She stepped onto the porch. "Oh," she said and extended her hand. "You're here."

But I wasn't touching anyone. "Stan," I said. After a moment, her hand fell.

She hugged her mother and then her dad, who pushed back her brown hair and whispered. Rachel nodded and turned to walk from the porch; then she whirled and her dress flared turquoise.

"I gotta nap." I glanced towards her father. What had she been doing last night she already needed sleep? "Later, I could show you around, if you're not too busy."

Since I knew no one and had nothing to do, I was in my room, attempting to read *Steppenwolf* for the second or was it the third time, when she knocked several hours later.

"Hey," she began. "Hesse, huh?"

I nodded.

"Still want to go out?"

I nodded again.

"You really got this tragic thing working."

When I didn't answer she shook her head and grinned, as if I were the retarded kid brother she'd been put in charge of. "Get a towel from Mary, you're gonna need it."

We drove south out of town. When she steered off the state route onto a secondary road that wound into the hills, she reached in her purse and produced a pipe and a baggie of pot.

"Pack us a bowl, why don't you? Or don't you smoke?"

"I don't," I said, though I did.

"What do you do? No, don't answer that." Her lips parted, a bright-toothed grin like John's. "It's time you learned."

I picked through the seeds and stems and filled the white onyx pipe.

"Careful," she said, when I held the lighter to the bowl. "There's no screen."

But I'd already inhaled the burning pot, coughed and spit, coughed and spit. With the second and third bowls I was more careful, and pretty soon my neck was stiff, which had been our euphemism, John's and mine, for getting high.

Hey Stan, your neck stiff yet? an echo of the first time we'd smoked and I declared, fearfully, that my neck was getting stiff.

"Leave me alone," I whispered.

"What?" she asked.

I shrugged. Sunlight like soldiers paraded through the trees lining the dirt road we'd turned onto. Country Joe and the Fish blasted on the radio, and for the first time in months I wasn't completely trapped in my own head, singing a song of woe. So much for sorrow, for heart-felt grief?

We parked, joining a still-life caravan: VW vans; rusty Pontiacs and Ramblers; Studebakers with psychedelic paint; gnarly-finned Fairlanes; and pick-ups with wooden bumpers and mattresses lining their beds.

"Where are we?"

"You'll see." She climbed out of the Bug, a towel draped casually over her shoulder.

Carrying my backpack—*Steppenwolf*, bathing suit, towel—I followed Rachel up the road, down a driveway past an abandoned farmhouse, then along a footpath which climbed a hill. The hedgerow we walked beside was choked with wild grape and berry canes.

"Try these."

Her palm cupped purple berries. Man, I wanted those berries, but not enough to touch her.

"Are they poisonous?"

She moved her hand to her lips and swallowed. "You've never tasted a blackcap?"

I shook my head.

"And now you've missed your chance, poor kid." She laughed, picked another handful and dropped them in my palm. "What do you think?"

Sweet and wild. "Far out."

"Far out," she agreed, her lips stained purple-berry red. We set out through thigh-high, golden-tipped timothy. The hill flattened, and we crossed a meadow headed for a pond enclosed by a semi-oval of trees. Music floated towards us. "Uncle John's Band," I think, but it could be memory playing tricks. John, John, John. Then Rachel reached up with both hands and pulled the purple dress over her head. Her tanned back emerged, dark hair falling past her neck and the wings of her shoulders almost to the dimples above the swell of her ass, which was briefly covered in white cotton panties. She hooked both thumbs in the waistband and wiggled bare, her bottom when it appeared as smooth and brown as the rest of her body. Rachel turned and faced me and though I tried not to look, my eyes fell from her tanned breasts to the tuft between her legs.

"Have fun," she said. My eyes, ears, my cheeks and neck burned with shame. "Let me know when you're ready to leave."

She ran towards the pond, where this tall freak with blond hair nearly as long as hers stood up and called, "Rachel."

She stepped into his naked arms. I glanced around and found myself in the inverse of a nightmare I sometimes woke from, the one in which I was naked in school, and everyone was pointing. *Killer.* For on that sunny Sunday there were maybe fifty people at that pond and except for me no one among the girls working all-over tans, the freaks with ponytails, or the little kids digging in the shallows wore a stitch of clothing. Not one of them looked my way as, red with rage and shame, I stomped off, fully clothed, to hide myself in the trees, swearing I'd never come to the Pond again.

III.

"Weren't you hot?" she asked many hours later, when we were driving home.

"Wasn't I hot when?"

"All those hours you didn't swim."

"How would you know?"

"I was watching for you."

She was right, of course.

"You weren't there the whole time, how would you know?"

She grinned. "You little spy."

"What's your boyfriend's name?"

"He's not my boyfriend."

"Whatever you call him. My old man. My main squeeze."

"He's not my anything. I don't believe in that old-fashioned possession shit."

The country road danced down the hill.

"He's just some guy you fuck?"

"You're really messed up, you know?" She looked at me and man, was she angry, man, was Rachel hot. "I don't fuck, I make love."

Then she wouldn't look at me, and night came on.

"I'm sorry, okay?"

She nodded. A mile or two later, I asked, "Who owns that place?"

"Everyone." Then, "Stan, I'm really wasted." She touched my forearm, and I swear, my skin blistered. "Would you mind driving?"

"I'll drive," I said, "only, don't touch me."

She pulled over and we climbed out. Cicadas sawed a summer melody. The air smelled sweet and drowsy. Somewhere in the woods there must have been another pond because a frog called, *Ribbit*, and a second answered, *Rabbit*. We crossed in front of the orange Bug in the blossomed dark and Rachel touched my shoulder.

"Don't!"

"You mean it?"

"You stupid or just trying hard?"

I climbed in the driver's side, slammed the door, and realized the Bug was a stick and all I'd ever driven was an automatic.

"We've got a problem," I said, when she sat down.

"We sure do."

"I've never driven a stick shift."

She could have laughed or said something cruel, and who would have blamed her? Instead, she answered, "It's easy, I'll teach you."

We bumped and sputtered down the road, and once, when she put her hand over mine to help time the shifting, I quaked, inwardly I moaned, but I didn't say a word. John was saying it for me.

"See," she said, when the Bug was in third and we were tootling home. "It's not so hard." *You don't know*, I thought.

"You want to talk?"

I knew what she meant. Not in a million years.

"That's cool," she said. "I'm gonna crash. When we get to Route 13, turn right. When we get to town, wake me up."

She closed her eyes and tuned out. She had an amazing ability and desire for sleep. Sleeper, that's what her father called her. Sleeper.

IV.

Our days assumed an easy rhythm. She'd sleep late, then we'd drive to the Pond. There were always kids, although some of the kids weren't that young. At night there were parties and live music in the bars. Our favorites were a place in Trumansburg called the Rongo, and two bars in College Town, where the Peabody and Zobo Funn bands played. Everyone would get wasted and spin around and dance in groups, which was fine with me, because it helped me ignore the voice in my head telling me what a fuck-up I was. Schmuck, asshole killer. After a few days people stopped asking my name, why I didn't swim naked, and why I wouldn't let anyone touch me.

Rachel was sleeping with several guys on a rotating basis, and often didn't come home when I did. Occasionally, she'd give me the car, but most nights, she'd drop me off, then continue on to meet whichever guy was that night's most lucky fella. I'd watch her taillights disappear and wonder what it would be like to be waiting for Rachel Bucholz to appear in my bed. Then I'd let myself in through the kitchen door, pour a glass of milk and steal up the back stairs, hoping I'd had enough to drink and smoke to sleep without dreams.

One night, after I'd been their guest about two weeks, I let myself in and Roger sat at the kitchen table, reading.

"Hi, Stan." He peered over his glasses. "How are you?"

He retained a slight accent, *ein bissel* German, a wee bit British.

"Oh, hi, Mister Bucholz."

"Is Sleeper *vith* you?"

I wanted to lie. He was her father, and she was out banging some guy. I shook my head.

"My daughter has many friends, doesn't she?"

In his eye, a twinkle, and on his lips, that dreamy smile.

"Yes," I admitted, "lots."

"Are you becoming friends?"

"I guess." I could feel myself turning red.

"You must *vonder*."

"What?"

"Let us not dissemble," he said. "There's too much in this world."

I looked at him. Light rebounded from his lenses. Mister Bucholz never struck me as the sort of man who would be friendly with my father.

"My daughter sleeps around." He smiled, but now it didn't strike me as quite so dreamy. "Sleeper."

I heard John's voice. *Pussy*. That was his favorite name. *You could get some of that.*

I said, "I'm not sure you have much choice, Mister Bucholz."

"Within parameters, we all retain choices." Roger closed his book. "You, Stanley, could have chosen not to live with us. I could tell Sleeper that if she chooses to be so liberal with her favors—"

I could feel myself blush again.

"—she may not live under my roof. But in times such as this." He smiled that goofy smile. "With so many damaged hearts, I think too much fucking is better than too little. Don't you agree?"

Agree? I could scarcely breathe.

"Please, sit." He motioned in that formal way he had. "Perhaps you would like a beer?"

"Just milk."

"Helps with sleep, ja?"

I nodded. Mister Bucholz walked to the fridge, poured a glass of milk and set it in front of me.

"Stanley," he continued. "Perhaps you could call your parents?"

"Did they ask you to tell me that?"

"Oh, no. They told me not to, it would make you angry." He had the strangest eyes. I hadn't fixed on their color until then, baby-blanket blue. "But I thought, since we are all becoming friends, I would tell you."

I sipped the cold milk. He said, "*When* I was your age, even younger, my parents sent me away. I was angry, just like you."

Pussy.

"Then we learned the Nazis had them, and I was even angrier. Oh, I had so much anger. I hated them for sending me away, I knew I could have saved them. Later, I hated myself for not dying with them. That was the worst anger of all."

The milk coated my mouth and throat. I thought I'd gag on that chalky taste. "What about the Nazis? Didn't you hate them?"

"Oh, the Nazis." He waved his hand. "Better to hate a stone. If I had not met my wife, I believe I would have died, I had so much anger here." He touched his chest and peered at me over his glasses with those impossibly blue eyes. I tried to see them as he described them, full of rage, but I couldn't. "So it's good to have friends, and I hope I have not presumed on our friendship to talk of such things. But I thought you would understand. Good-night, Stanley."

The next day it rained, slow and drenching, and we didn't go to the Pond. At noon, Rachel still hadn't emerged from her room although I knew she was home because the orange Bug was in the driveway. I knocked on her door. When she murmured, I stepped inside and stood beside her bed.

"Hi, Stan," she said, one eye barely open. "I got in really late."

She snuggled down, her cheek a blossom against the pale pillow.

"Would it be okay if I watched you sleep?"

She sat up and tucked the sheet around her. "You want to lie down with me? No touching. Just sleep."

I tried to imagine what that would be like, the sound of her breathing, the scent of her hair, so little space between us I saw John's eyes winking out. *You, pussy.* I heard her father, *My daughter has many friends.*

"Can't I just watch?"

"I'm not sure I can sleep that way."

"Can't you fucking *try?*"

She lay down and closed her eyes Her chest rose and fell; her lips relaxed. I watched Rachel sleep, really watched her, and loved her like I'd never loved anyone, not even John, my oldest and best friend, who was better than me at everything. I hated myself for that, too.

From then on, when Roger and Mary left for work, I'd slip into Rachel's room and sit in the chair beside her bed. Her eyes frolicked beneath her lids; I wondered whom she dreamed of, Rachel Bucholz, whose favors were her father's secret plan to save the world. *I have given you my only daughter.* When I tired, worn out by my own sadness, I'd move to the floor, lay my cheek against the side of her bed and fall asleep. That's how she'd find me.

"Oh, Stan," she'd say, "you're such a goof."

Then we'd dress, drive to the Pond and our day would begin.

V.

When I'd been there almost a month my parents called one Sunday morning and announced they wanted to visit. No, I said, it would be too awful, but Roger and Mary came on the line and said, Of course. Later, Mary prepared an elaborate brunch. Homemade waffles with pecan pieces enriching the batter. Raspberries from canes in their own back yard. Fresh whipped cream. Some sort of fat English sausage. Halfway through the feast, Rachel drove up and joined us on the screened porch. She sat across from me, between her parents at the small oval table, rubbing sleep from her eyes.

"Uh-oh," she said, looking around. "What's wrong?"

Roger asked, "Why must something be wrong?"

"When Mary breaks out the bangers and the waffles, something's always wrong." She glanced at me, but I wouldn't meet her eyes. "All right, Mom." She flipped the hair off her face. "Who fucking died?"

"You have a filthy mouth," Mary said, and turned to Roger. "You see how she talks to me?"

"A filthy mouth and a filthy body." Rachel glared at her small, refined mother. "Now, what the fuck is going on?"

Roger and Mary looked at each other across the table. Mary's lips were thin and white, I suppose with rage. I didn't know, I never much considered what Mary felt.

"Stanley's parents are visiting next weekend." Light exploded like rockets from Roger's glasses. "Is that so terrible?"

"Depends what Stan thinks, doesn't it?"

They turned towards me, and I saw clearly, if nothing else, that I could not please them all. As to what I really thought or felt, I could not access that for years.

"It doesn't really matter what I think, does it?"

Rachel smiled. "It does to me."

"Of course," Mister Bucholz said. "Of course, it does."

"Let them come." I stood. "I'd like to be excused." I walked smartly from the porch into the house.

For the next week, relations were strained between Mary, Roger, and me. I see now that wasn't fair. But Rachel and I were closer than ever. I wanted to tell her what happened. Describe my dreams, how I sometimes felt when John died he'd somehow moved inside me and that was his revenge for ending the life that was certain to be better than mine. *Hey, pussy*, he'd whisper, or I would, who knew who said it? I'd cram my fingers in my ears, squeeze my eyes so tight. *You look stupid, you know that?*

The night before my parents arrived, Rachel and I were driving home from the Pond. It was just dark, not quite nine, and the cicadas were singing.

"Are you going out again," I asked, "when we get home?"

"I don't have to."

So that night we stayed in. We smoked pot in the yard and went to her room and played Scrabble. Around midnight, she produced a piece of hash she said she'd been saving for a special occasion, and we smoked that, too. In kind of a daze, we sat on her floor with incense burning, our backs braced against her bed.

"Tell me," she said, "what was it like?"

I was so stoned her words banged together and echoed. "What was?"

Her eyes were pools I could drown in. She moved her mouth to mine. Someone else moved my hand.

Oh no, I cried, I can't.

Do it.

"When your best friend died."

I rolled off her and banged my head on the floor.

"Stan, please don't. Just don't."

When I tried to bang my head again, she grabbed me and held on.

I said, "John wants to make love to you."

"*John?*"

"He says he can't and it's my fault. So I have to."

"That's really not funny."

I didn't answer.

"You want me to make love to you because your friend died?"

"Because he never got the chance." I could barely see her beside me in the milky light from her window. "Because it was my fault."

"It was an accident."

"I wanted to hurt him."

"Oh, Stan," she said. "Not like that."

"Please."

"Why should I?"

"Because I'll love you forever."

"What a line." She closed her eyes and shook out her hair all around. "I would have slept with you anyway, Stan, you're such a sweet guy. All you had to do was ask."

In the milk and coffee shadows of her room, she smiled that bright-toothed smile. "I'll be right back." She walked to the door; the lock turned. Then I followed her to the bed. "Tell me about John."

"He was tall and blond. We were friends since we were six. He was better than me at everything."

"No," she said. "I don't believe it." She began to unbutton my shirt. "Did you love him?"

I nodded and felt a sob rise and fall within me. Then she was kneeling above me, pulling her dress over her head.

"John, if you can hear me, I will make love to you, too, but you have to promise to leave Stan alone after this." Her head popped free of the dress and dark hair tumbled around us. "Do you promise?"

If John answered, I didn't hear him. We were bathed in sweet light. I closed my eyes and kissed Rachel and felt her kiss me. And when she helped me inside her, she called me John and Stan and John and Stan and held me when I came and afterwards when I began to cry.

"It's all right," she said. "He's gone now."

The next day when my parents arrived, I announced I was ready to go home. When Rachel and I said goodbye, I whispered into the hair above her ear, "I love you."

"Not really." She stepped back and smiled. "But thank you."

It's been thirty years now and I'm sitting alone at my desk

waking from the dream I sometimes have, the one in which we're at the Pond for the first time. She lifts her dress over her head and the years fall away down her tanned, unlined back. I wish I could speak to her now and thank her. For she was wrong and I was right. I have always loved her, faithful as the night. And John? My dear friend John has never left.

Mark Weiss, photograph

GREG KOSMICKI

Windows

> Which is easier, to say,
> "Your sins are forgiven,"
> or to say, "Rise and walk"?
> —Luke

At my office the new cube
I moved into has a brick wall
on one side and no windows.
I am not terribly unhappy here
just desperate. Desperate for something,
something that is not
on the computer screen. Something
trees, and wind. I've noticed
the reflection of the fluorescent
ceiling lights makes two little
window-like pictures on my screen
when my computer has what the
computer people call the "desktop"
showing—no desktop at all
of course, like everything else
on the computer, it's virtual—
a simulation of whatever's
there. The reflection of the lights
is real and the smears
from my fingertips—one looks like
a head, almost, a silhouette,
but all the rest of them look
like clouds, the effect
heightened by the fact
that the fluorescent's bluish
color against the green
quote unquote desktop
makes the reflection, real
as it is, a blue sky blue,
a cerulean virtual sky
like looking through a window
in the roof. It might look like

the hole that Jesus saw
when those desperate friends
of that desperate man
lowered him to the healer
through the hole they'd broken
in the roof. Who does that
make me like? Jesus, or the sick man
lying on his pallet in his rags,
lowering slowly down into
the midst of the crowd,
gripping the sides of his cot
like a man destined for
greatness or agony? I know
I am not the healer,
I must be the paralyzed man
and that makes more sense—
for here am I
not in my body
before the computer.
So I let myself be lowered
and each time I fall
on rags held by my friends
into the presence
of the one who can heal,
I look up and see
the sky, sky so azure
it breaks my heart,
clouds like fingertips of rain,
and fall into that healing sky lost
somewhere, out on a prairie
by an abandoned grade, boxcars
of sky clanking past, a two-car
train filled with sky
my fingerprint clouds holding
the sky inside together, yellow
buttercups, daisies,
tall grass, wind, and I lie
here on this floor, meadowlarks
calling to me the world's first name.

Dripping Faucet

But what I was mostly
thinking about that drip drip drip
was how over the course of time
it can wear away the hardest stone
and I was wondering why
it is our sink doesn't have
a hole or two in it.
All the nights we've lain in bed
listening to it tap on the stainless steel
like some guy trapped in an elevator
until one or the other of us
finally gets up and
breathing words through teeth about
someone's holy mother come to the kitchen
to twist the left faucet
just so, to slow
the drip to maybe once a half-minute.
Once a half-minute times
one drip times one hour times
one day times—well, you
do the math. It's staggering!
Just the weight of the water alone!
Why is our house even standing?
I'm twisting this faucet
and I'm thinking of that old
organizing song *step*
by step the longest march
can be done
can be done
many drops can turn the wheel
singly none
singly none,
twisting this faucet and I'm thinking
this dripping is a lot like writing poems—
how many poems written
by how many poets times
how many mornings by
how many nights will
it take to wear away even just a bit

182

of one Ku Klux Klan member's hate,
one Nazi's, one dumb idea.
I'm twisting this faucet and listening
to the drip of the water as it
thunks against the steel
like a raindrop on an army helmet.
Listening to crickets
out there in the dark,
thinking how many crickets
how many summer nights
how many years. . . .

NINA CORWIN

Orpheus Rebounding

When Orpheus gets back to earth, his rescue mission
an abject failure, he flogs himself bitterly for that one wrong turn.
Eurydice is back in the hot arms of Hades
and he is pathetic as a raisin, all the juice wrung out,
his parade of wailing animals bringing up the rear.

Back at the condo, he has nothing for comfort but his old lyre,
growing frumpish and dingy from disuse.
The wood nymphs come ringing his doorbell, beseeching him
to serenade them with vicarious love, that golden tongue
of the good old days. But he hasn't got it in him
and soon they give up and drift away.

Eventually, however, and for want of anything better to do
he picks up the neglected instrument, listlessly begins to finger
the strings and as he does, he remembers how he'd play Eurydice,
sometimes pull her hair back, pluck at the harp of her
the notes she would make forming a sweet Oh.

As in Oh, the openings to all things delicious
Oh, the berries and melons of her flesh, Oh, the way she'd rise
and fall to his touch, and even just plain *Oh*.

And as his fingers remember, the notes come trickling out
like honey from honeycomb, and the forest catches its breath.
The animals and the wood nymphs draw near
and soon he's got his groupies again,
like Eurydice back in the days of the smoky blues bars.

He concludes the gods have given him a gift indeed
counts his blessings: how they could have grown bored
with each other, fallen out of love
and there she'd be—like an empty cereal box
but not as easy to dispose of.

Instead, she is beautifully dead and he is free.
Free of the tarnish and clutter, the dank and musty corners
free to clean house and remember them together, brimming
and spotless, free to start over basically just plain free.

Something in his rusty loins begins to hum.
He looks to see a woman smiling.

Mark Weiss, photograph

MAX FREEMAN

Myrtle and Laurel

For once, Adam doesn't know
what to say. What to call her.

She nips at his neck—quick, pleasurable
bee stings. This has never happened before.

She was combing her hair,
reflecting by a lake as calm and cool

as God, when he found her and brought her
here to this nook beneath roses and towering

jessamine. But he doesn't know what to do with her.
There are no books on this. There has never

been a woman like this, all softness and grace,
her virtue apparent everywhere.

He won't look at her; he bats dour
eyelids over downcast eyes. But he isn't afraid

because she won't say no. He runs a hand down her
arm and tries his tongue. His blood

sours as it runs, turning him from pure
docility to something savage.

She giggles as if she already knows the procedure,
as if she practiced in his absence.

Her Premonition

My curly hair and the bite of the brush.

The tug of the teeth and the cold water on the hot morning skin of my face.

The air on the cold water and the pink of sunrise freezing the mountains.

The bleak mountains and the bleating of reeking sheep.

What dark god's voice, in every patch
of wind blundering to and fro, up and down
the desert landscape? He—my father: no prophet,

as oblivious to coming disaster as his stupid
children and wife. On the trail, a snake striking
harmlessly at my feet and then retreating
into the bushes. My sigh of indifference;

the stillness of the bluish air. The sound
of a ram fleeing in the thicket; the inexorable
sun rising over trees and beating the dirt
into the path. All of this was sentence.

Not because I wandered to the leather
tents of the sons of men, ran my fingers
through their ochre hair. My innocence;
or my willfulness. Not because I forgot
any daily task, flagged at the prospect
of devotion. Not for the ear I inclined

to the voice of some hungry god,
whose reckless brag would send
more than just my family to the slaughter.

Not even vengeance for a father's sins,
but a sacrifice to his consuming righteousness,
perfect, patient and white-hot as molten ore.

She Sang Beyond

Through utter and through middle darkness borne
With other notes than to the Orphean lyre.

Nobody would notice the graveyard
dark of the path, the rough of it, the gravel
and dirt length of it, the silent stretch of it.
Her bright eyes turned these things over
as she passed, impelled by some secret

to continue. Her footfalls disappeared
noiselessly into the dim timeless dream.
Who wouldn't notice the loud parade
preceding her—one man, though the noise
of his song echoed over the sound

of her measured steps. He wasn't listening
to discern if she followed—though his face
was screwed up in an incredible
grimace. He was listening—to his lyre,
how the world sang back to him. As if sadness

were something he could name, own, slip
into his pocket. This was his idea of love. He thought
to save her, prove his gift. Nobody would notice
her white hands tucked into the dark warm folds
of her dress, the slow pace of her, the sweet gray shade

of her. She couldn't hear grief playing
in his song. The display didn't register
or draw her along like love. Other notes
lulled her, darker: a dirge, the feel
of her own voice in her throat, pomegranates

split wide and set on a stone table. Nobody
could have made this song but her.
Nobody would take notice of her secret tune
which led him up the steep path, which sent
him like an arrow shot from night

toward morning. He never even realized
she was singing, though he obeyed her. When
he stood a jubilant, anxious silhouette
against the garish gates, she stopped her song
abruptly. She might as well have called to him.

Mark Weiss, photograph

CHERYL DUMESNIL

When

I used to believe in signs:
    the ocean leaving something
        brittle and unbroken on the sand

for me to find, or the fog horn
    I heard from my dark bedroom
        after you told me to listen

hazy mornings before dawn,
    that low moan guiding minor
        vessels away from craggy

harm. If there were
    guarantees in love, then
        yes, I would follow you

to New York City, Puerto
    Rico, a place of birth, yours
        or mine. I used to believe in

tides pulling bodies toward
    unknown purples and deep,
        deep greens—that a dream

about blue whales signified
    desire, terrifying and good, rising
        in the body after a decade-long

fight. Back then I would track
    a barn swallow's crooked path
        across an August-drought field,

expecting cattails and water
    to emerge from the earth,
        and they would. When I

believed in signs, a coyote
        pawing at dry brush, her tail
                a flag among weeds, told me

I should look for you,
        and a black-tailed deer
                holding my gaze meant:

if I could find you, you would stay.

Lucy Aron

Mysterious Object of a Lucid Verb

I'm scrambling eggs or pumping gas
when they tumble out. From the heart,
if not the tongue. Like a bell. More music
than prayer. Then the careening train
chugs to a stillness and I remember.

For a wisp of time I remember, and all
the white noise of my life — the jangle
of people, traffic, work, or doubts and longing —
morphs into a star. I become sky.

Daily this bell, like grace. The words ring
and You're near. I remember. This breath.
This meal. This day. "Thank You."

Moving Toward Fifty

This storm is serious. Three days
and still it snows, a foot at first,
big flakes, iridescent, thin as mica,
a steady sugaring two inches
every day. There's always too much
weather here or not enough,
but there is less and less to want
when snow shuts you in.
I move from room to room,
hungry and I don't know what for,
not a book or cupboard that can feed me.
Time is a country of large, open spaces
I can't quite get my arms around.

Before Desire

Men carry inside them the story we are never told,
of Adam just before sleep
in urgent discourse with God.

Desire came later, offered in the apple's seeded star.
But first there was this desperate bargain
struck to cure the thing he could not name.

The last he saw — God's hand coming at him sideways,
a fist of dream scorching his belly, the clean
snap of something torn from him forever.

Against this rough seam of loss, women are thin ribs
of light, knowing the way bones do, by ache
and prescience, how hard men try

to keep from us how much they wanted this.
Curiosity — a stitch in the side,
the first fever — before knowledge, before desire.

Erika Mikkalo

Discovered Pupae

> Has found out thy bed
> of crimson joy,
> And his dark secret love
> does thy life destroy.
> — *William Blake*
> *"The Sick Rose"*

Yes *never*, yes soft tidings, yes old Persian rugs
that convey some worthy past. Yes clay, yes red
Wine, yes scratched sepia image or black-and-white
at some cultural debacle
          or happening
                    or event
where you will be identified as Unknown. Yes long fall
(We took it to the bridge), yes open path
shining, yes new praise (a shocking
surprise). Yes the present. Each moment
newly stillborn. Each moment
an insect in amber. Each moment a
present, a gift, a given,
The gifted. A yard and a
Garden. A man spading over earth
and listening. A small stream and Girl
Scout troop on the sidewalk with their potentiality of campfires and
Boxes of sweets. Yes the certainty of some new
Grace. Yes a peach under the moon. Yes elders.
Yes poems about bones, yes stop signs.
Yes crazy baby calls out yes or to God.
Yes B. Yes V.
Yes 'm.

Known Bluebottle

With Blue-uncertain stumbling Buzz —
Between the light — and me —
And then the Windows failed — and then
I could not see to see —
— Emily Dickinson
"Poem No. 465"

See *now*, see easy dance, see invisible
steps choreographed in air. See filth, see the
empties, see the emptiness in the eyes
slickly depicted in a Polaroid or as mirthless
stones in the doughy "O" of a bar booth's joke photo strip, black
and white. See winding roads (miles to go
before you sleep), see infinite rest (a fine and
private place). See hope (the
thing with feathers, the comedian's nephew).
See hopelessness every second that you
permit it entry. See an infinite
Void, a storming black pit that you carry
in your heart and your gut,
not trust, only the darkest cravening
Fear. A gangway but not a blossoming
courtyard. A man lingering but
not loitering. Elevated trains and a quiet
ceremony, in a sense, in the park but not a
memorial or commemoration. Seen the proof of a definite
beginning. Seen an apple core and the
waxing moon. Seen ancestors.
Seen legends regarding ancestors, seen witnessing shotgun barrels, heard
Testifying lead.
Seen corpses, unnamed, unclaimed, unnumbered.
Seen three. Seen 12.
Scene X.

DANIEL POLIKOFF

Ingress

How the sense of the animal
    alters
        when the wild
            breaks into your home. The field

mouse hurrying about in the meadow is
    a fine fellow
        industrious
            co-worker prey to all sorts of heaven-sent

disasters; but when he eats the Indian corn
    that adorns
        the season table
            stashing the stolen grain behind the piano,
              buffet and (even

as you're reading) the bedroom bookshelf
    the rogue's
        a thief of
            peace. And when, out of nowhere, the Great

Blue Heron whose lithe height and lightning
    force
        thrill
            in the marsh appears on your own brick

courtyard, stalking toward the fountain filled with
    glimmering
        koi
            how much more keenly you know his

sharp beak, and how much more deeply take in
    the quick
        spear-slash
            skewering your golden heart.

DEREK SHEFFIELD

Wildlife

When I am silent enough
for a hermit thrush to suddenly be
worming his thin beak
down a mottled, half-lifted wing

inches from my elbow,
for a fox to step through
yellow grass the way a wave
would wash past my shins,

my reach, in plume and curved
claw, air and earth, extends.
And the dead in their pooling
stillness, their perfect wonder?

SARI ROSE

Communion

When Sam came home that evening he saw on the steps of his front porch a stranger laughing into a cell phone. He parked the car in the driveway and looked at the person laughing. She registered with him as a strange woman, but at the same time he was replaying something he had just said to his boss; something about looking beyond the fat in a fat person when interviewing one. His boss claimed not to understand what that meant. "How do you look beyond fat? In this case we had a woman who was big enough for two. If you looked beyond one, you saw the other. Two in one. Two sets of gum."

"One gum," Sam said. "One person. One fat person."

"Two people. Okay two, *equal* people, but one is a ticking liability."

"One gum, though," Sam had said, and then the boss said he had to go, which meant Sam had to go, too. So he went home. Now he was sitting in his car thinking about a fat woman who couldn't get even one shift at the fish counter. And thinking that after the boss had said gum, Sam couldn't top him with anything better.

Sam got out of his car and walked to the front of his house. The stranger on his porch was a young woman who sat like a man, her legs spread and confident in loose jeans. He knew he didn't know her and he knew Sunny didn't know her. The woman had a side top tooth that rested on her bottom lip and short blond hair that looked unwashed. He gauged how he would walk by her, confident, casual; it was his house, yet as he walked past her he felt shy. She had big thighs.

Sunny, his wife, was standing by the door looking out. Sam said, "Excuse me," to the woman, who didn't seem to notice him, even when he had to step over her arm outstretched on the top step. "No, not just candy corn and wax lips," she said into the phone. "I feed them other things. Chicken, noodles. Come get me, Paul, I'm hungry."

"Who's she?" Sam whispered to Sunny as he walked in the front door.

"My God, Sam, I know. She's so sad." Sunny was whispering because they were in the front foyer, close to the front door where the woman was. "She's a mother I run into at Peasley School."

Sunny's whispers were full of faint hisses and ∂ sounds — the sound of someone chewing and popping gum. He couldn't understand what Sunny was saying and tried, instead, to read her face — her light brows rising, the slight bulb at the tip of her nose turning red.

"She walked by the house as I was shaking out rugs." Sam didn't get it. He had the idea of putting his whole head into her mouth to understand her. "What?" he said.

"She said her car is broken and her hip is smashed. She unloads steel doors at Home Express and a steel door fell on her."

"Why's she on our steps?"

"She was on pain meds because of the steel door crushing her hip. The meds made her high and she crashed her car. Now she's walking home from the body shop."

"Why's she on our steps?"

"She's trying to make it home. I told her to sit and I'd bring her a soda." Sunny had her hand on his shoulder and had her mouth to his ear so she could whisper. Her breath was like a yellow buttercup. He thought of girls putting buttercups under his chin and asking, "You like butter?" He loved butter.

"What are we going to do with her?" he asked.

"I'll give her a soda and offer her a ride."

"So, get the soda."

"I don't know if we have any soda."

"Then what are you going to give her?" All the whispering made him realize he was dry, thirsty and likely had bad breath. "Do I have bad breath?" he asked her. "No," she said in a breathy whisper. He loved that he could ask her if he had bad breath, and later ask her for butter. He could say, *Do I smell? Am I dirty?* And she'd smile and always say, *No.* Or, *No* with a swooning roll of the eyes, as though she was ready to keel over from the smell of dirt. But he couldn't whisper more questions now because the whispering was hard on his throat and he was thirsty. He wanted to talk normally. He wanted dinner. He wanted the kids to go to bed and he wanted to tell Sunny about the fat woman and the boss. "What are you going to get her?" he asked, this time above a whisper, almost full voice.

"Shhh," she said, "Diet Lemonade. With a lot of ice."

"Then get it." He was getting angry now. He walked from the foyer into the dining room where he put his briefcase on the table, his jacket on the back of a chair. Sunny went into the kitchen and opened one cabinet after another. Then she opened the refrigerator, but he couldn't see her because she was on her knees, probably sticking her whole head in and looking at the slotted shelves from below.

He walked part way into the living room to say hi to the girls but they didn't say hi back. They were watching TV, Rae sitting cross-legged on the linty rug, Jayney standing before the set. Rae was wearing a white diaper and a white turtleneck with red stains down the front. She looked to Sam like a bare-legged butcher. Her thumb was in her mouth and, as always, the thumb struck him as a breast. Rae had loved Sunny's breast and now she loved her own thumb. Breast and thumb were the same to her and he understood that, since he himself was a breast and thumb man. He didn't suck his thumb anymore, but with a file and clippers he groomed it a lot.

Next to Rae, his six-year old, Jayney, was moving to *The Simpsons*. She was bending at the waist, bobbing wildly, and she was pumping her arms and hands over to her right side. With her head and torso bobbing, she might have been mimicking an Orthodox Jew; but with her arms working off to one side, she could equally be rowing a canoe. The big giveaway was her lips, puckered as though waiting for a kiss. And, also, Lisa Simpson playing the sax.

He walked toward the far end of the living room toward the TV. "Hi?" he said. Rae didn't take her thumb out. She didn't even look up. Janey shook her head from side to side, as someone blowing into a sax might signal a hi.

He finished his circle around the downstairs, going into the tiny pantry area and back into the kitchen. His shirt, he noticed, had ink on it. He had an anxious feeling, almost panic, that he was a white shirt with ink. The shirt was walking and the shirt's heart was beating fast. He had the idea of giving the girls each a pen and telling them to write on him. Maybe they would have a rare, insightful thought that he was inside.

He didn't say excuse me to Sunny as he leaned over her to pull out a beer from the refrigerator. He knew he was rude, but he was at odds with his boss; he was hungry and tired; and a stranger, camped out and comfortable on his porch, was the object of Sunny's attention. To streamline his stress and make things easier on himself, he decided to be mad at Sunny. "You gonna find that lemonade or what?" he asked.

The phone rang. It was Sister Anne from across the street. "There's a woman sitting on your porch," said Sister Anne.

"Yes?" said Sam.

"I know her. Do you know her?"

"Sunny says her kids go to Peasley School and Sunny knows who she is."

"How much does Sunny know about her?"

"All I know is we're looking to give her a cold drink because her car broke down and a steel door fell on her."

"I know her son, Franklin, from communion," Sister Anne said. "If you need any help let me know."

From the other side of the refrigerator, still hidden from view, he heard Sunny saying, "For the love of dirt!"

"Do you have a Coke?" Sam asked. "Sunny wants to give her soda or lemonade."

"We always have some soda around."

"Could we borrow some?"

"I'll bring it over."

Sunny came into view. From her squatting position, she put her arms behind her and leaned backward, so she was nearly on her back in front of the refrigerator. Sam gave her a hand and helped her up. "Ouch!" she yelled and he realized he had pulled a little too hard.

"Who's she talking to on the cell phone?" Sam asked.

"Someone who's amusing the heck out of her. She seems to be acting coy and come-hither."

"On our porch?" Sam asked.

Sunny shrugged and put up her hands as if to say, It's out of my hands.

"Does she live near here?" Sam asked, but was afraid to know. "Is she a neighbor?"

"She's desperate and pathetic. Of course she's our neighbor."

Now he was angry at Sunny for saying that someone who lived near him was desperate and pathetic. For so much as saying he made a bad choice with this house, and anyone who lived in a two- to three-mile radius was a recognized deadbeat.

"Where's she live?"

"The other side of Spring Street. She was married to this nice mixed guy. They're not together anymore but she sometimes sleeps there, on the sofa, so she can get the kids off to school in the morning. She herself is staying with some woman, who I think takes care of her."

Sam felt she had this information and was bullying him with it. He shook his head and felt the very top of his skull, the crown, aching and throbbing. In books, you always read about a throbbing penis. But it was his head that throbbed. It often throbbed, especially at work. Eventually, he thought, the pain would work its way down and his penis would have the headache. One day, he'd be at work and blurt out, "Man, my penis has a throbbing headache."

"Tell me, again, exactly why she's here?" he asked.

"Her car, her hip. She's poor, she's close to homeless."

"You know her whole story," he said. He said this only because he thought it was the end of the story. He wanted the story to end. But Sunny had more.

"One time she asked if I could give a ride to her little boy who has child care at the Y. Her car was in the shop and she had no way to get him there. The boy sat in back in Rae's car seat and she sat in front."

"Where was Rae?"

"Child care."

He wouldn't say, "We pay money for Rae to go to child care so you can take this other kid to child care?" Instead he said, "So, you are now the designated driver, Young Lady." He tried for a tone of humor, with an undertone of nastiness.

The doorbell rang and it was Sister Anne. "I have Sunkist Orange," she called out. "Do you have a glass and some ice?"

"Come in," Sunny called.

Sister Anne came in, a tall, six-footer of a nun, and Sunny gave her a hug. "How you doing?"

"My knees stink, but otherwise I'm okay. You have a glass?"

Sunny started getting everything together and the sister said, "Do you know who this girl is?"

"Who?" Sunny and Sam said together

"I probably shouldn't say."

"We won't tell anybody," Sunny said.

"Who would we tell?" Sam said.

"Okay, but don't say I said. Her name is Francesca. She lit a match and burned one of her kids, little Akeem. She didn't tell me this. What she told me was she was mad at him because he got her

202

into trouble with the Y. They scolded her because Akeem wasn't wearing socks and the Y has a sock rule. The kids have to wear socks because they take off their shoes in the day-care room and they don't want them barefoot. Francesca claims he had socks when she brought him, but he took them off. She was afraid they'd report her to the state for the socks. She thought that might be considered abuse. So what does she do? She burns him. She gets mad at him for the socks and lights a match or a lighter and burns his leg. The state took him away and put him in a foster home and she can go visit him."

"Oh, great," Sam said.

"How badly was he burned?" Sunny was now holding a glass filled with ice and orange soda.

"A blister burn. Second degree. He took off his Band-Aid and showed everyone his big blister during circle time."

"Who's Paul?" Sam asked.

"Beats me."

Sunny took the glass of orange soda to the front door and with her free hand knocked before she came out. Sam and Sister Anne watched her. Francesca looked up at the soda being handed to her, but didn't stop talking and didn't seem to say thank you. Sam saw Sunny talk to her and Francesca put her hand over the phone and answered Sunny back.

Sunny returned to the kitchen. "She'll take a sandwich. And some tomato soup."

The sister said, "You feed her and she might not ever leave."

"What can I do?" said Sunny. The three of them were standing in front of the refrigerator. It made Sam sad that whenever the sister came over, they always leaned or stood, never sat. For one thing, the kitchen was too small for a table and chairs. For another, time in this home was never leisurely. It was always food, dishes, diapers, clothes, dance, dance, dance, dance till you drop. Sometimes, and especially now that it was October, they could take a bike ride to the funeral home.

"Let's chip in and give her money for a meal," said the Sister.

"I don't know her," said Sunny. "She might use the money for drugs. Oh, and she doesn't have a car."

"Damn, you're right," said Sister Anne. She hugged her arms to her chest. "OK, tell her you'll feed her and call her a cab. Don't drive her anywhere. And I'll pay for the cab."

"I'll pay for the cab," said Sam. "But you know what?" He paused. "Could you hurry with that sandwich, Sunny? I want her gone and you know, frankly, I'm hungry too."

"Of course you are," said Sister Anne. "The man has to eat. Hey, look. You could come over to our house for dinner. Sister Anne Sullivan is making a roast."

Sam pictured a nice china plate, a glass of wine, the evening news on the large screen. The sisters' home was a spiritual place. Always warm, always a piece of cake for dessert, the cross on the wall, Jim Lehrer on TV.

"Wouldn't that be nice!" said Sunny. She looked to one side. "Warm roast. Meat."

"Remind me to tell you about the meat man," Sam said, hoping to get Sunny's attention.

"The meat man from work?" Sister Anne said. "You still having trouble with that guy? Send him over here."

He loved Sister Anne. He wanted to sit down at her table and tell her about the meat man, the fish man, his boss, and the fat applicant. "I love roast," Sam said. "But we have a guest on our porch and we can't leave." He could smell the roast now on Sister Anne's large block of a white blouse.

"I'll tell you what," Sister Anne said. "I'll bring you two over a plate. Have the kids eaten?"

"Yes," said Sunny.

"Frankly," Sam said, keeping his voice low and looking around. "I want this woman gone as soon as possible. I don't want everyone driving by seeing her sitting on our step talking to Paul. It looks like our house is turning into another rooming house."

"That's all we need," said Sister Anne.

Across the street from Sam and Sunny and next door to the Sisters of Mercy was a rooming house. Forsaken men lived there. They sat on the wide porch steps, in full view, broadcasting their various stages of pickling or psychosis. When Sam looked out his living room window, he didn't see lawns or trees. He saw these men, sitting on the porch. It killed him.

Ten years ago, when Sunny and Sam had bought their house, the rooming house was an elegant, commanding single home, a 1920's colonial with full front porch and ornate columns. But the couple who lived there divorced and the house was bought by a wealthy rooming house scion. He converted the single family into single rooms, each room occupied by a disabled man on state assistance. The roomers were thirty-, forty-, fifty-year-old men, acting as though they were on their own for the first time and seeing what they could get away with: pissing outside and seeing if mom would come out and yell; drinking 7-UP out of a paper bag and baiting a cop to stop. "Only 7-UP, Officer. Sorry for your inconvenience." Sam had been mowing his lawn once when he saw this happen. After the cop left, the guy called to Sam, "Hey, I'll do this for one month then switch to gin. Got to train these guys." Sam didn't look at him, but gave him a wave of the hand. The wave meant, "I'll graciously ignore you, if you pretend not to exist."

There was the roomer who took discarded stuff Sam had put on the side of the road—old chairs from college, broken bookcases, supermarket drinking glasses given to him by his mother—and sold them at his weekly tag sale. There was the guy, all hair and bones, who spent hours sitting motionless at the edge of the rooming house sidewalk. He had a long spindly beard that came down to his chest and the sisters called him "Moses." Sam called him Mr. Shit-In-His-Pants.

"Look, you guys sit tight," said Sister Anne. "Sunny, make Francesca a sandwich and I'll be back with your dinner."

Sunny kissed her cheek and Sister Anne said, "We'll take care of Miss Tough Nut. Don't worry. You'll get your dinner and she'll be gone by 8:00." Sunny and Sam escorted Sister Anne to the front door and opened it for her. Sister looked down at her feet, careful where she placed them. She looked like she was navigating rocky terrain on the Northern Slope. She looked worried she might step on Francesca, who was now semi-reclined on the step and saying just then, "You gonna take me out for dinner, Paulie?"

Sister Anne gave Francesca a little wave, a low hand wave, as she tiptoed around her, and Francesca took the phone away from her ear and said, "Is that you?"

"It's me," said Sister.

"From Saint John's?"

"That's me." Sister paused at the base of the porch and wrapped her arms around herself.

"Sister Somebody?"

"Sister Anne."

"Right. Franklin really likes you."

"He's a cute little boy. So eager to please."

"He's my dear baby boy. He's very important to me."

"I'm sure of it, Hon." She waved to Francesca as she walked down the front walk to the street. Sister waited at the edge of the walk until two trucks and a motorcycle passed. Sunny and Sam watched her from the front door as she crossed the street and made it safely to her own home.

"Paulie, guess what?" Francesca said into the phone. "The nun from communion was just here." She put one leg higher, close to her chest, and draped an arm around it. "Hey, she lives across the street here. I didn't know that. It's a regular house. Two story. I thought they lived in a nunnery. Hey, Paul. Get thee to a nunnery."

Sunny left to make the sandwich and Sam stood near the door, listening to her, watching her drink her soda.

"I graduated high school," Francesca said into the phone. "I left home and I finished on my own. With honors. You didn't know this about me, did you?"

Jayney came to the door, still holding her imaginary sax and bobbing like a pecking chicken, her lips still ready for a kiss. Sam kissed her and said, "You didn't say hi."

"Who's that?" Jayney said, lifting up the sax and pointing it out the front door.

"Someone Mom knows," Sam said.

"Who is she?" Jayney asked.

"I told you, I don't know. Someone Mom knows."

"Mom, who is she?" Jayney called out.

Sunny walked into the foyer and said, "Shhh. She's a mother and a sad person. Come away from the door."

"What's she doing here?" Jayney said.

"That's my question," said Sam.

"Shhh," Sunny said, from her dark spot in the foyer. "Her car is broken. She's been walking all over town. Her hip is hurt and she's hungry."

"I don't know what you guys are talking about," said Jayney. "I want to ride my bike."

"No one is leaving the house," Sam said, "Until that woman is gone."

Jayney started to cry. "Why can't I go outside with my bike? Who is she?"

"Sunny, I want her gone," Sam said.

"I'll hurry with the sandwich."

They all left the door and went into the kitchen. Sunny brought out a skillet, started heating it with butter. The butter made Sam hungry, but not for sex. Just for butter. A grilled cheese sandwich. Sunny nuked some soup and put it on a tray, along with another glass of orange soda.

"Lucky her," said Sam, standing in the kitchen door. "Maybe I should sit on the porch and act down-and-out. Maybe I'll go talk to Paulie."

"Excuse me," said Sunny, looking disgusted, pushing him away from the refrigerator so she could open it. She brought out more butter. Sam didn't know if she looked disgusted because of Francesca or because of him.

Sunny had the sandwich on a tray now and walked through the dining room to the foyer. Jayney and Rae were together now standing by the front door. Rae's hair looked sweaty. The two girls stared at the tray, wanting to know who the woman was and when she was leaving. "Everyone give me some space," Sunny said, as she walked to the front door.

"That sandwich looks good," said Jayney. "And we never get tomato soup. You never make *me* tomato soup."

"Everybody step back, please," said Sunny. "Go back in the living room. Sam, take them into the living room. Or better yet, go upstairs. Start their baths."

"We never get anything on that tray, either," said Jayney. She was standing right at the front door, watching her mother stop in the dining room for a napkin. "Where'd you get that tray, Mommy? I didn't know you had that tray."

"Paulie, they're bringing me a tray with food," Francesca said. "They're better than you. I don't even know them and they're bringing me food."

"I want to go outside," Jayney said. "It's too early for my bath."

Rae stood by her sister's side, sucking her thumb. Her diaper looked low and full and with one hand she was fingering a little bit of fine hair above her ear.

"Sam," Sunny said again. She sounded edgy and militant. "Get them upstairs, please. And baths!"

He was starving and didn't want to start baths. Baths weren't supposed to come for another hour. There was supposed to be dinner and a bike ride to the funeral home. That was the routine and that's what he wanted. Then he saw Sister Anne leaving her front door carrying a big tray covered with various things wrapped in foil. He didn't want to leave his food. It would be here any minute. He wanted to count the seconds it took her to cross the road.

Sunny knocked on the front door slightly with her foot, so Francesca would look up and open the door for her. As Francesca stood up, Sam could see how broad she was. She had a manly frame, big shoulders, big boots. She wore a white button-down shirt tucked into jeans and her waist was small, her hips big. "Sam," Sunny said in a normal voice. "Could you please take the kids upstairs?"

"My dinner is coming," he said. Sister Anne was crossing the street now, looking both ways for cars, holding the tray tightly.

"You have food coming for me, from both sides," said Francesca. "Look at the big tray the nun is carrying. It's fucking Thanksgiving here."

"That's for me," Sam said. He was holding the door partway open and talking to her. "Sunny's tray is for you."

"Which is better?" Francesca said. "Don't I get to choose?"

Sam couldn't tell if she was trying to smile or smirk.

"Well, the one coming across the street is for me and Sunny."

"Sunny, is that your name? You drove me to the Y that time and I never knew your name."

"Her real name is Margarite," Sam said. "We only sometimes call her Sunny. Like when we're hungry and she's busy."

"You messin' with me?" Francesca asked.

"He's joking," said Sunny. "Don't spill the soup," she said to Francesca. She pointed to the items on the tray. "I have grilled cheese, soup and soda."

Sister Anne was on the sidewalk now looking at her feet again and trying to navigate her way up the porch stairs. Sam opened the door, pushed by Sunny, and walked down the steps with his arms outstretched for the tray.

"Wait a minute," said Francesca. "Hey, excuse me, Miss Nun. Who's that tray for?"

"For Sam and Sunny."

"Her name *is* Sunny. What's this Margarite shit? You were messin' with me. You think I'm stupid. I don't need your fucking food. Forget it." She sat down on the porch steps and resumed talking to Paul. "These people are fucking with me. Come get me.

Let's see." She stood up and looked back at the house at the pillars and the mailbox. "368 High Street. Come fast. I'll wait."

"You're not going to eat the food?" Sunny said.

"You messin' with me. I ain't eatin' nothin' you got to give me. Thanks anyway. Unless I eat the nun's food. I'll eat her food."

"No way," said Sam. He had gone past her into the house. He stood behind the door, holding the tray, and spoke to her through the glass. "Sorry but I'm hungry too."

"Look, I'll eat the grilled cheese," said Sunny in a soft voice, bending down low to Francesca, as though whispering to her now. "And you and Sam can split the roast beef."

"I ain't sharin' nothin' with him," she said loudly.

"Sorry, Hon," said Sister Anne, "These people are nice enough to let you stay here till your ride comes, but they're hungry too. I brought the tray for them."

"Let them have it," Francesca said. She pushed over to one side of the steps and turned her face toward the shrubs.

"I'll stay awhile," said Sister Anne.

"Thank you, Sister," said Francesca. She pulled out a pack of cigarettes and shook one out. As they all watched her, she also took from her breast pocket a lighter.

"Can you not do that here?" Sunny said. "The cigarettes and lighter upset my children."

Francesca said nothing but stood up to put the cigarettes and lighter back in her shirt pocket. When she finished putting them in, she patted them and smoothed the pocket. She began to sit down again, but then whirled around fast and in one ferocious move punched the door. The glass shattered and made a screaming pop. Sam stood there watching her. He went to put down the tray on the floor, but she opened the door by the handle, her hand bleeding, and punched the tray out of his hands. Foil packets flew, and juice sprayed out. A foil-wrapped ball, looking like a big silver egg, hit Rae's bare foot. She kept the thumb in her mouth but opened her mouth around it and screamed. Saliva ran down her chin, onto the same stained shirt. Inside the front hall, his hands free now, Sam grabbed Francesca, who had crossed the threshold, and pinned her arms to her side. She was squirming and twisting but he was taller and in a rage equal to hers. "Open the door," he said in a restrained fervor to Sunny. He was trying to keep his voice as low as possible, so the girls wouldn't get further panicked. As he brought her outside he said, "Sorry, Sister," to Sister Anne who had to back away to make room for the struggling pair. "Call the police, Sunny," he said.

He got Francesca down the steps, hugging her with all his might. He wanted to bloody her mouth and nose, to pummel her, but instead put all his strength into a massive squeeze. He brought her to the sidewalk, not knowing what to do with her then.

He looked across the street and one of the rooming house guys, the tag sale magnate, was watering potted plants he had lined up on the porch steps. "Need some help, man?" shouted the guy.

"I'm okay," yelled Sam.

"I'll come over."

"Christ, that's all I need," Sam said under his breath.

"Me too," said Francesca, who was rocking her shoulders with enormous strength and making furious attempts at breaking free. Sam got her to the ground and was not so much restraining her as hugging her. She was hitting him and he could do nothing, it seemed, but hug her.

The guy crossed over to the sidewalk and looked down at Francesca who was writhing under Sam and hitting his back while arching hers, trying to throw him off. The neighbor stood there for a moment, then said to Sam, "Let's divide her, Buddy. I'll take the bottom, you take the top." Sam moved over, and gave the guy a spot. The neighbor sat at her feet, put her legs over his, and leaned over using all his weight, a paperweight move, Sam thought. A heavy brick on a sheaf of blowing papers. Sam moved to the top of her head, linked his arms like a rope through hers and pinned her elbows against the sidewalk. He liked to think it was a wrestling move, but he had never wrestled, had never really fought. And here he was, playing cowboy and steer with a stranger outside his doorstep.

"You call the cops, buddy?" the neighbor asked Sam.

"Yeah."

"They come fast. We'll just wait. Hey, if you keep it up," he said to Francesca, "I'll sit on you."

"Paul's coming to get me," Francesca said, still squirming. "He'll get here before the cops."

"Paul," said the tag sale guy. "Paul? Paul coming? Good. We'll take him out, too."

Behind him Sam heard Jayney and Rae crying. He heard

Sunny say, "It's okay. It's okay. The woman's getting help." He heard Sister Anne said, "Don't worry, girls. She's harmless." And Sam, aware now of a drumming in his head, was grateful that his neighbor had come and taken Francesca's lower half, the part with the bad hip. He didn't want the bad hip, but he wanted the hip damaged. He closed his eyes and could only feel his arms straining and the hardness of her muscles. He didn't have enough strength in his position to crush her, though he wanted to crush her, wanted blood to come out her nose and mouth. He was close to her mouth and the thought came to him that he could smother her, he could put his fist in her mouth and smother her, roll her on the ground, roll her down the sidewalk, down the street, trying his best to put her out.

BARBARA PRESNELL

Saturday night, your mother has a date

but you don't. You sit on the blanket chest
behind the dressing table, watching her dab
concealer over shadows, rose blush
on olive cheeks, something blue across lids.
On her nightstand, the FM radio plays

the Eagles, fading in, fading out.
You want her to hurry up and go
so you can have a cigarette and then another
and another on the back porch steps,
get the six-pack from your cold car trunk,

finish the last half of joint you've been saving,
fall asleep in front of the TV, past
the National Anthem, when she won't
be home, your mother,
who washes the gray from her hair

each month, can't hold her wine,
cries by herself in the night. She's in her bra
and panties, sliding hangers across
the metal closet rail, holding skirts and slacks
to her frame like paper-doll clothes

when Paul McCartney breaks in —
*You'd think that people would have had enough
of silly love songs.* She sings along
in her tiny voice, her fleshless hips
bumping air, silky underwear flapping,

and you can't help but get up
from the chest and do the descant
when Paul does, bumping your blue-jeaned
behind into hers. You raise your arms
like flamenco dancers, twirling from the vanity
to the telephone table and out the door
to the hallway, until, you don't say it

but you know you are in this together,
and when the doorbell rings,
neither of you will be ready.

Voices

In pink slippers, not quite touching ground,
she wanders from the kitchen where she sipped
her last water for the night, through the den,
cutting heat and lights, to our beds,
where we lie sleeping.
She tucks quilts beneath our chins
to catch our dreams, kisses cheeks
(mornings I wake to her scent on my pillow),
then slips under blankets with my father,
their voices wafting back to our rooms.
I make out *roast beef, yard,*
other parent words, and sometimes
my name, *Barbara . . . Barbara,*
working its way down the hallway to me.

Summer nights, when we play
for hours in the yard,
sometimes the Boogeyman
creeps in my window,
squeezes through the tiny squares of screen,
and hunches beneath my bed
waiting for silence which does not come.

I cannot imagine the dawn I will wake
to my father's awful retching,
my mother by the bathroom door,
Is there anything I can do?
his mumbled, lost response.
Or the night The Cough will climb
into her bed and grind her throat,
two o'clock, three o'clock, four
o'clock, five o'clock.
Or the day I will hear *roast beef . . .*
yard . . . Barbara . . . in each creak of floor,
heavy cat paw, breath of wind on glass.

CELESTE WOOD

By what should I measure time?

Milkweed vines knot themselves

along the lines of old fences,

give up their white silk
to mosquito evening.
The genuflecting willow tree
each year stoops closer to her roots.
Once along the river bank,
I dug for clay with small fingertips,
I picked burs from my socks.

The underwater dreams,

the dreams of flying,
differences hardly noticeable:
the way light breaks itself
into weedy lines,
or rests its spine on edges,
the horizons,
the receding darknesses.

BRITTON GILDERSLEEVE

Ca Dao Việt Nam: Vietnamese Folk Poetry, by John Balaban, 2003.Copper Canyon Press, P.O. Box 271, Port Townsend, WA 98368. 74 pages. $15.00 paper.

The background and context for John Balaban's newly revised translation of Vietnamese oral folk poetry, *Ca Dao Việt Nam*, can be found elsewhere in this issue, in his moving essay "Getting Beyond the War." Discovered and recorded in the midst of war, these quiet poems contain all the ellipsis, profundity and evocation of natural beauty of the better known Japanese poetic forms *haiku* and *tanka*. Short and deceptively accessible on first reading, *ca dao* bear reading again. And again, and yet again, as the spare form releases the music, imagistic power and wisdom given new voice through these sensitive and respectful translations.

Balaban has done an elegant job of both selection and translation. In his discussion of *ca dao*'s strictures, he notes the internal rhyme, the syllabic constraints, and the ways music augments and intensifies the Vietnamese language's own musical inflections. While a reader can only imagine the *ca dao* sung (unless we also purchase the accompanying CD), theVietnamese originals printed beneath Balaban's translations highlight the delicate balance he has achieved between accurate translation and lyric poetry, finding equivalents in English for complex tonal nuances.

> When the rice fields lie fallow,
> lying on the back of my buffalo, I play the flute.
> People are happy with a Thuân-Ngiêu king
> whose bright mind spreads over land like the wind.
> The Lô waterfalls are clear, free, and high.
> We shake off the jacket of the dust of life.
> "Harmony in the Kingdom"

The history of the Thuâ'n-Ngiêu period may elude a reader, but the happy boredom of minimal activity, the security of national peace, and the rejuvenating qualities of cold clear water are familiar blessings. They woo a reader today as surely as they must have seduced a listener hundreds of years ago.

Other poems are equally compelling. Balaban discusses "The Sàigòn River" in his introduction, but the poem needs little explanation: ". . . the rice shoots gather a fragrance,/ the fragrance of my country home,/ recalling my motherhome, stirring deep love." Any expatriate knows the way the fragrance of food grown in home soil transports you back to the land itself. The French even have a name for it: *terroir*, the taste of land held within the food grown there. At its best, translated poetry offers a reader a comparable taste of a culture.

Walter Benjamin once said that the best translation asks not that the original be translated into the language of the reader, but that the mind of the reader be translated into the spirit of the original. When you close the final page of *Ca Dao Vietnam*, your spirit may well feel translated half-way around the world, half a millennium ago. In *Ca Dao Vietnam*, Balaban offers us at least an onlooker's seat at a continuing feast, sometimes joyous, sometimes poignant, a feast that celebrates an enduring Vietnam, one too rarely glimpsed in the West.

About the Authors

ANH CHI PHAM was born in Vietnam, grew up in Southern California, and went to school in the eastern U.S. She has worked as a business analyst and marketing manager, but has now traded a business career for the writing life. She is embarking on a novel and pursuing her MFA at Antioch University.

NANCY ARBUTHNOT, translator of Lê Pham Lê, teaches poetry and creative writing; her original poems and translations have been published in *Shenandoah*, *Calyx*, *Willow Springs*, and other little magazines; *Mexico Shining*, a book of her versions of Aztec songs, was published in 1996.

LUCY ARON's work has appeared in *Rockhurst Review*, *Many Mountains Moving*, *The Phoenix*, and *Dogwood*, among others. A writer of prose and poetry, she received The Santa Barbara Arts Fund Individual Artists Award first prize in literature for non-fiction; one of her poems was nominated for the Pushcart Prize.

HARRY AVELING is Head of the Indonesian/Malay Program at La Trobe University, Melbourne, Australia, and Adjunct Professor of Southeast Asian Literature, Ohio University. His recent anthology *Secrets Need Words: Indonesian Poetry 1966-1998* (Ohio University Press, 2001) was shortlisted for the 2003 New South Wales Premier's Prize in Translation. He has taught on behalf of La Trobe University in both Hanoi and Ho Chi Minh City.

JOHN BALABAN is the author of eleven books of poetry and prose, including four volumes, which together have won The Academy of American Poets' Lamont prize, a National Poetry Series Selection, and two nominations for the National Book Award. In addition to writing poetry, fiction, and nonfiction, he is a translator of Vietnamese poetry and a past president of the American Literary Translators Association. He is Poet-in-Residence and a professor of English in the creative writing program at North Carolina State University in Raleigh.

WILLIS BARNSTONE has published work in *Southern Review*, *New Letters*, *The New Yorker*, *Harper's*, and *Prairie Schooner*, as well as a profile appearing in the fall 2003 issue of *Poets & Writers*.

LAURA CASTELLANOS is a Cuban-born writer now living in San Francisco. Her poetry has been published in the anthology *My Lover is a Woman*. She has also co-authored a book on financial planning for Latinos, *Latino Book of Personal Money Management*.

JUDITH CODY has won poetry awards from *Atlantic Monthly* and *Amelia* magazines. Her poems have appeared in *Eureka Literary Magazine, Central California Poetry Journal, Sequoia*, and *Stonecloud*. Her book of poems, *Eight Frames Eight* (2002), is illustrated with her pen and ink drawings. She has completed a book of poetry, *The War Memoir*, on her life in Japan during the Vietnam War contrasted with her father's service in World War II.

PATRICK COLE's work has been published in the *High Plains Literary Review* and nominated for inclusion in the Pushcart Prize anthology. His work has also appeared in *Amelia* and *The Black Bear Review*. He lives in Spain.

NINA CORWIN is the author of *Conversations with Friendly Demons and Tainted Saints* (1999) and co-editor of the anthology *Inhabiting the Body: A Collection of Poetry and Art by Women*. Her work has appeared or is forthcoming in *Spoon River, Spillway, Mid-America* and *Comstock* Reviews.

BARBARA CROOKER's poems have appeared widely in journals, including *River City, Poetry International*, and *Passages North*, and anthologies, including *Thirteen Ways of Looking at a Poem*. She has published ten chapbooks of poems, most recently *Paris* and *Greatest Hits*, and has won many prizes, including the 2003 Thomas Merton Poetry of the Sacred Prize. Recently, Garrison Keillor read three of her poems on NPR's *The Writer's Almanac*.

DIANE SHIPLEY DECILLIS's poetry has appeared in *The MacGuffin* and *New York Magazine*, and is forthcoming in *Eclipse* and *Rattle*. She is owner and director of an art gallery in Southfield, Michigan, and the author of the website MonaLisaMania.com.

DU THI HOAN, born in 1947 in Hai Phong into a family of Chinese origin, is now the Chief of Poetry Committee of the Hai Phong Union of Literature and Art Associations. Her published works are *The Small Path, The Genesis as Pre-School*, and *The Light Between*.

CHERYL DUMESNIL's poems have appeared in *Calyx, Many Mountains Moving, Bakunin, Barrow Street*, and other literary magazines. With Kim Addonizio, she co-edited the anthology *Dorothy Parker's Elbow: Tattoos on Writers, Writers on Tattoos*. She currently teaches private workshops in the San Francisco Bay Area.

SUSAN ELBE's chapbook, *Light Made from Nothing*, was published by Parallel Press in 2003. Her poems have appeared or are forthcoming in *Calyx, The North American Review*, and *Passages North*, among other journals, and in the anthology *A Fierce Brightness: Twenty-five Years of Women's Poetry*. In 2002, she won the inaugural Lois Cranston Memorial Poetry Prize.

D. M. FERGUSON works in a psychiatric office in Rochester, New York. The poem in this issue is Ferguson's first publication.

MAX FREEMAN is currently a poetry reader and intern for *Quarterly West*. His work has won an Honorable Mention in this year's *Atlantic Monthly* Student Writing Contest and his poetry has appeared in *Gulf Stream*.

GAIL HOSKING GILBERG's book, *Snake's Daughter: The Roads in and out of War*, was published by the University of Iowa Press. Her poems and essays have been published in such places as *The Fourth Genre*, *Tar River Poetry*, *The Florida Review*, *The Chattahoochee Review*, and *The Threepenny Review*.

BRITTON GILDERSLEEVE teaches at Oklahoma State University, where she also directs the Oklahoma State University Writing Project. Her work has appeared in *Spoon River Poetry Review*, *Florida Review*, *Crab Orchard*, and *Cimarron Review*, among others. Her chapbook *The Privilege of Breath* was published by Pudding House in 2003. A reader of poetry for *Nimrod*'s editorial board, she uses the commute from Tulsa to work at OSU to daydream of returning to her childhood in Southeast Asia.

ERIC GOODMAN is the author of *In Days of Awe*. He is director of creative writing at Miami University of Ohio and has taught at the Iowa Writers Festival.

MICHAEL L. GRAY, writer and photographer, lived and worked in Hanoi in 1995 and from 1998 to 2001. His photo-essays and stories about Vietnam will appear on his new website, www.michaelgray.ca.

HO ANH THAI currently works in Vietnam's Ministry of Foreign Affairs and is the elected Secretary General of the Hanoi Writers' Association. Best known in the West for his novels *Behind the Red Mist* and *The Women on the Island* and his short story collections *Fragment of a Man* and *The Goat Meat Special*, he has published sixteen novels and story collections.

WAYNE KARLIN is a novelist, the American editor of the Curbstone Press Voices from Vietnam series, and a professor of languages and literature at the College of Southern Maryland. His latest novel, *The Wished-For Country*, was published by Curbstone Press in 2002. He has published five other novels, including 1999's *Prisoners*, which won the Paterson Prize in fiction, and a memoir. He is a veteran of the Vietnam-American war.

ANDREW KAUFMAN's *Earth's Ends*, the book-length manuscript containing "The Temple of the Jade Emperor," won the Pearl Poetry Prize and is scheduled to be released in fall 2004. His chapbook, *Cinnamon Bay*

Sonnets, was published by the Center for Book Arts after winning their manuscript contest; his poems have appeared in such journals as *Atlanta Review*, *Beloit Poetry*, *Rattapallax*, and *Spoon River Poetry Review*, in addition to having earned Honorable Mention in *Nimrod*'s Pablo Neruda competition in 1995.

MELISSA KOOSMANN is a student in the MFA program for poetry at the University of Arizona and Editor-in-Chief of the literary magazine *Sonora Review*. She has poems forthcoming in *Blackbird*.

GREGORY KOSMICKI is the editor and publisher of The Backwaters Press. His most recent chapbook is *The Patron Saint of Lost and Found*, published by Lone Willow Press.

ANDREW LAM is an editor at Pacific News Service. He is working on his first short story collection. Lam is featured in *My Journey Home*, a documentary from WETA on his visit to his homeland, Vietnam, to be aired nationwide on PBS stations in April 2004.

LAN CAO, Boyd Fellow and Professor of Law at William and Mary Law School, is the author of *Monkey Bridge*. She co-authored, with Himilce Novas, *What You Need to Know About Asian Americans*.

LE PHAM LE, born in Dalat and educated in Saigon, left her country with her family at the defeat of South Vietnamese forces. Her book of poems, *Gio Thoi Phuong Nao/From Where the Wind Blows*, was published by the Vietnamese International Poetry Society in 2003.

LY HONG ANH's divides her time between Seattle and Vietnam. Her story in this issue of *Nimrod*, "Hair and Homeland," is her first publication.

GARY MAGGIO's recent poems appear or will appear in *Reverb*, *Bryant Literary Review*, *Rio Grande Review*, *Steam Ticket*, *Poetry Motel*, *California Quarterly*, *Sea Change*, and *Salvage*.

DEBRA MCCALL is an interior designer and feng shui consultant in the Tulsa, Oklahoma, area. Her work has been published in such journals as *Potpourri*, *Byline Magazine*, and *Crosstimbers*, and received an Honorable Mention in the *Nimrod*/Hardman Awards 20 competition.

MICHAEL MCCOLLY is working on a memoir that chronicles his travels through several countries affected by the AIDS pandemic. Parts of his memoir have been published in *Ascent*, *The New York Times*, *Salon*, and elsewhere.

ERIKA MIKKALO's writing has received the Tobias Wolff Award for short fiction from *The Bellingham Review*, among other honors. Her poetry was recognized in the finals of the 2001 Poetry Center of Chicago's Seventh Annual Juried Reading and received the Millennium Poetry Award from the Writers' Publishing Cooperative.

ERIN MURPHY was a finalist for the 2003 *Nimrod*/Hardman Pablo Neruda Prize for Poetry. Her work has appeared in *The Georgia Review*, *Field*, *Kalliope*, and *Nimrod*, among other publications. Her poetry manuscript *Science of Desire* will be published by Word Press in June 2004.

PAULINE T. NEWTON's poem, "On This Dreary, Moonless Friday," appeared in *The Graduate Review* for The American University. She is currently working on an article on Jenny Boully's *The Body*, a poem composed solely of footnotes, for which she will interview Boully.

MARTIN OTT's story "Nick's Place," in this issue, is part of his manuscript *Perishables*, stories from which have appeared in *Cimarron Review*, *Connecticut Review*, *Pacific Review*, *Phoebe*, and elsewhere. He was a finalist for the 2003 Agha Shahid Ali Prize in Poetry.

PHILIP PARDI has published poems, translations, and an essay in recent or forthcoming issues of *Mid-American Review*, *New Orleans Review*, *Borderlands*, *Seneca Review*, and *Quarterly West*.

PHAM DUY KHIEM (1908-1974) was born in Hanoi and educated in France. He was one of the better known of his generation of Vietnamese Francophone writers, owing largely to his lecture tours, literary tours, literary prizes, and governmental posts. Pham's collection *Legends des Terres Sereines*, first published in French in 1951 and republished in 1989, won the Prix d'Indochine. A supporter of the Republic of Vietnam and its Ambassador to France from 1955-57, he published essays, memoirs, other collections of legends, and the novel *Nam et Sylvie*.

DANIEL POLIKOFF is a poet and teacher. In addition to writing poetry, he lectures on classic German literature, especially Rilke and work stemming from the Parzival legend. He has completed a translation of Rilke's *Sonnets to Orpheus*, six of which have been published in *The Chariton Review*, and is at work on a book on Rilke.

BARBARA PRESNELL has published three collections of poetry: *Snake Dreams* (1994), *Unravelings* (1998), and *Los Hijos* (2002). She received a 2001-2002 North Carolina Arts Council Fellowship in Writing. Her poems appear or are forthcoming in *The Southern Review*, *The Malahat Review*, *Cimarron Review*, *Rhino*, and *Tar River Poetry*.

SARI ROSE has taught writing in public schools and has worked in marketing communications and university development. Her stories, published in *The Iowa Review* and *Nimrod*, among others, have earned recognition; she won *The New Millennium* Prize in Fiction and took second prize in the 2002 *Nimrod*/Hardman Katherine Anne Porter Prize for Fiction.

DEREK SHEFFIELD won the *North American Review*'s 2003 James Hearst Poetry Award and was a finalist for the 2003 Elinor Benedict Poetry Prize. His poems have also appeared in one chapbook, *A Mouthful of Thumbs*, and several other journals, including *Poetry Northwest*, *Puerto del Sol*, and *Poet Lore*. His interview of William Stafford's family, "Talking Recklessly," appeared in the Spring 2003 issue of *The Seattle Review*.

ELIZABETH KELLER WHITEHURST was a finalist in the competition for the 2003 *Nimrod*/Hardman Katherine Anne Porter Prize for Fiction.

CELESTE WOOD lives in Nevada City, California. Besides writing, her greatest passion is for ecology. She writes mainly with the hope that all humans will come to know they are part of a universe, one creature among many.

ABOUT THE ARTISTS

MICHAEL L. GRAY, whose essay and photographs appear in this issue, is building a new website, www.michaelgray.ca, where more of his stories and photo-essays about Vietnam will appear.

ANH DAO KOLBE, born somewhere outside Saigon, came to the U.S. in 1972, a year after her (adoptive) mother found her as a 6-month-old at An Lac Orphanage. She left two years later and grew up with her Greek and German parents in the Middle East. After attending boarding school in England, she returned to the U.S. for college. The photographs in this issue of *Nimrod* emerged from her 2-month backpacking journey of return to Vietnam last spring.

JAMES TUONG NGUYEN earned a degree in Fine Arts from Northeastern Illinois University and is working on a portfolio of documentary photographs recording the social conditions of Vietnam's poor. He has revisited Vietnam and traveled to Cambodia and Korea to study Vietnamese people working and living there.

FRANCISCO TOLEDO, an artist from Mexico, has exhibited his prints internationally. The etching in this issue comes from a limited edition portfolio, *Trece Maneras de Mirar un Mirlo*, 1981, including ten drypoints and a Spanish translation of Wallace Stevens's "Thirteen Ways of Looking at a Blackbird."

VU HOI, artist, poet, photographer, and teacher, created the calligraphic texts for the poems of Lê Pham Lê in this issue. An internationally recognized artist, Vu Hoi has exhibited work in France, Italy, the United Kingdom, Germany, South Korea, the Philippines, and the United States. His poetry, written in Vietnamese, has been translated into other languages, including *Poems in White Color*, in English.

MARK WEISS is an ophthalmologist in Tulsa and an award-winning photographer.

Nimrod International Journal

The 27th Nimrod/Hardman Awards
The Katherine Anne Porter Prize for Fiction
& The Pablo Neruda Prize for Poetry

First Prize: $2,000 Second Prize: $1,000

Postmark Deadline: April 30, 2005

No previously published works or works accepted for publication elsewhere. Author's name must not appear on the manuscript. Include a cover sheet containing major title and subtitles, author's name, full address, phone & fax number. "Contest Entry" should be clearly indicated on both the outer envelope and the cover sheet. Manuscripts will not be returned. *Nimrod* retains the right to publish any submission. Include SASE for results. The results will also be posted on *Nimrod*'s Web site in June 2005: www.utulsa.edu/nimrod.

Entry Fee: $20 includes both entry fee & a one-year subscription (2 issues). Each entry must be accompanied by a $20 fee. Poetry: 3-10 pages. Fiction: one short story, no more than 7,500 words.

- -

To subscribe to Nimrod:

Please fill out this form and send it with your check.

$17.50 for 1 year, 2 issues (outside USA, $19)
$30 for 2 years, 4 issues (outside USA, $36)

Name_____

Address _____

City_____ State _____ ZIP_____

Country _____

For more information, to submit, and to subscribe:
Nimrod/Hardman Awards
The University of Tulsa, 600 S. College, Tulsa, OK 74104
918-631-3080   nimrod@utulsa.edu   www.utulsa.edu/nimrod